BIOGRAPHY

BIOGRAPHY

A Brief History

NIGEL HAMILTON

HARVARD UNIVERSITY PRESS

Cambridge, Massachusetts • London, England

2007

Printed in the United States of America

Library of Congress Cataloging-in-Publication Data

Hamilton, Nigel, 1944–
  Biography : a brief history / Nigel Hamilton
    p. cm.
  Includes bibliographical references and index.
  ISBN-13: 978-0-674-02466-3 (alk. paper)
  ISBN-10: 0-674-02466-4 (alk. paper)
  1. Biography as a literary form.   I. Title.
CT31.H36   2007
907.2 22   2006051132

For Sophie Hanna Hamilton,
née March 29, 2006

Contents

Illustrations

BIOGRAPHY

Prologue

Biography—that is to say, our creative and non-fictional output devoted to recording and interpreting real lives—has enjoyed an extraordinary renaissance in recent years. Not only has it become, in the West, the dominant area of nonfiction broadcasting and publishing, from television to the Internet, but it is now one of the embattled front lines in the struggle between society's notions of truth and imagination.

Why, then, has so little been written about the nature, history, interdisciplinary pursuit, cross-media expansion, and ethics of biography? Why is there in print no single, accessible introduction to the subject, either for the general reader or the specialist?

For the past ten years I have been teaching the history and practice of biography. *Biography: A Brief History* is intended to give readers a narrative overview of biography's modest origins in prehistory and its long development in the West, culminating in its explosive growth in the late twentieth century. The book attempts to give some of the reasons—social, psychological, economic, technological—that biography has reached such prominence, only a hundred years since it was relegated (in the *Oxford English Dictionary*) to inferior status as a sub-branch of literature, devoted to the lives of individual *men*. In sum, I argue that the pursuit of biography, controversial in its challenge to received ideas of privacy and reputation since ancient times, is integral to the Western concept of individuality and the ideals of democracy, as opposed to dictatorship or tyranny.

I also argue that the term "biography" needs to be redefined to encompass the many, many different ways in which real-life depiction is practiced in Western society. (For reasons of economy I have had to limit my survey, in the Christian era, primarily to the English-speaking nations.) For students of biography in the West, the late seventeenth-century coinage of the word "biography," as a term for literary rather than graphic depiction, was understandable; that century, after all, was an age of rising literacy and of lexicography. The conception of the word and its dictionary definition was unfortunate, however, for it narrowed, rather than expanded, the public notion of life depiction. "A biography" became the correct dictionary designation for a written record of a particular human life, but it was not distinguished from the more generic term "biography"—the latter thus being limited only to *written* lives, rather than including the entire field of real-life human depiction, in various media: a noble field that stretches back to classical times and beyond.

The result, for scholars of biography, was disastrous. Instead of becoming, like "history" or "art" or "literature," a premier domain of the humanities and sciences, "biography"—with its newly restricted boundary, encompassing only written, documentary records of human lives—seemed insufficiently substantial or scientific to merit study or teaching, a fate that became self-perpetuating. Lacking scholars to examine it, and constrained by a focus so narrow that no student could be made sufficiently curious to learn of its history, biography's integral role in the shaping of human identity, as well as its varying practice through the ages across different media, went uncharted and largely ignored.

This unfortunate error (one that allowed other disciplines to sniff at "biography" as under-theorized and—

heaven forbid—"popular") has now stretched to the point
of absurdity in this, the West's third millennium. Today, in
one of the greatest paradoxes in Western civilization, biography is the most widely practiced and often the most controversial area of nonfiction broadcasting and publishing,
pursued across every artistic and informational medium,
and a mainstay of democratic practice in the West. Yet
while universities abound in departments devoted to research and the teaching of subjects as diverse as journalism, hip-hop, women's studies, sports, and African American studies, to name but a few, the subject of biography—
which connects all of them—has no major department devoted to its study at any single university in the world save
in Hawaii![1]

This narrative is therefore designed to sketch, all too
briefly, biography's long history and controversial status in
the modern Western world, but also, in doing so, to address—in an all too preliminary fashion—a significant la-
cuna in the academy, in order that those who practice, enjoy, or use biography, and are interested in the study of the
individual, can gain at least some idea of how biography
first began; how it then developed as a human enterprise
involving many media, not simply writing; how the depictions of the lives of real individuals evolved in the Western
world; and how, in the mid-eighteenth century, Samuel

Johnson came to his great vision of modern biography and its importance to modern Western society. We will also see how that admittedly Anglocentric vision was then recast in Victorian times—and with what results. And how, belatedly, in the twentieth century, biographical output in the Western world has not only exploded into a variety of new media, from film and radio to television and the Internet, but has crossed a hundred borders—borders of discipline, social morality, the law, politics, gender, genre, and artistic expression.

Finally, we shall look at where we stand with biography at the start of the third millennium. We'll review what seems to be happening in the Western world of real-life depiction, expressed in different media, ranging from official print biographies to questing television documentaries, from reality-TV programs to celebrity supermarket tabloids, from contested memoirs to Internet blogging. We'll look at motives, markets, rules of engagement, and both the local and larger social significance of the pursuit of biography—seeking to address its benefit, and its deficit, to our Western culture today.

Last, we shall examine where biography may be heading in the future—in the brave but not unthreatened world of the individual.

CHAPTER I

Evolutionary Biography

*D*epictions of the animal world by human beings go back tens of thousands of years, to the
time when the species *Homo sapiens* first began to record its
own existence. Vast, vivid cave-wall renderings of the great
beasts of nature, on which and beside which early humans
lived: these still have the power to awe us, yet they are puz-
zling, too.

Why *did* our early forebears paint themselves so unreal-
istically—as matchstick men—in comparison to their eer-
ily impressive representations of wildlife? What was the
purpose of such paintings, applied deep inside their cav-
ernous quarters? André Leroi-Gourhan, the great paleon-
tologist, felt that the self-portraits of Paleolithic men and

1. Perhaps the first graphic depiction ever made of a "real-life" human drama: a prehistoric hunter wounded by a bison, painted on the Shaft Wall of the caves at Lascaux, Dordogne, Southern France, ca. 15,000 B.C. *Copyright © The Granger Collection, New York.*

women—especially the cartoon-like sculptures of faceless wide-hipped females—were produced as part of a symbolic representation of the sexes that had already existed for thousands of years—and were thus, inevitably, idealized and ritually decorative rather than attempts at realism.[1]

The matchstick men of European cave painting are one puzzle. Painted Egyptian mummies, thousands of years later—though thousands of years still in *our* past—present

another. Those gaudy Egyptian caskets, with stylized, ste-
reotypical depictions to help prepare the deceased for his
or her journey to the afterlife, give no sign of the unique
individuality or distinctiveness of the swathed mortal inside—yet in late Egyptian antiquity, following Greek fashion, we sometimes find a tantalizing painted portrait of
the deceased: an artistic monument to his or her unique-
ness *as an individual,* often down to the tiniest human detail or blemish.[2]

Biography as Window on the Ancient World

However little we yet understand early records of individual human beings and the motives for their depictions, we
treasure them, for they tell us about the culture in which
they were produced—something that alerts us, perhaps, to
one of biography's most important and ongoing functions
today: *its crucial contribution to our knowledge, understanding,
and reconstruction of past civilizations.*

Is the value of biography, then, its historical window
onto a past culture? And if so, how did such representation, as a biographical agenda of early societies, develop—
and why?

While we cannot know the answer, we do know that
virtually all early societies and civilizations have sought to
record themselves through the *memorialization* of distinct

individuals, often in poems and songs which were handed down from generation to generation. For anthropologists, the significance of such biographical, often genealogical, legacies lies in the importance of *identity:* the fact that people in social groups derive their sense of belonging, and thus cohesion and confidence, from their sense of personal connection, kinship, and inheritance. This sort of meme-heredity, as we might call it, came to comprise a vital transmission of culture from one generation to the next—no less important, in its way, than practical forms of knowledge, whether firemaking or flourmaking. *Knowing who you are* is, for humans, a fundamental aspect of living; and to a considerable extent that knowledge must depend on knowing who others are, and were, too.

Ancestor worship, bloodlines, and other modes of tribute paid to past members of a society have thus characterized *all* ancient cultures—indeed, still mark both tribal and "sophisticated" urban communities today. The "commemorative instinct," as biographical historians call it, seems to be a powerful concomitant to genealogy: a psychological, possibly evolutionary drive.

Individuality

Tracing the "commemorative instinct" through human history, we can certainly peep into the lives of our ancestors, as social historians and archaeologists. As *students of biography,* however—that is to say, the study of *individuals* in society—we can indulge in a further search of our own. For it is our very curiosity about individuals *as individuals,* rather than as nameless members of a society, that suggests another clue to biography's fascination today—at least in Western civilization.

Today we in the Western world value *individuality* as never before—perhaps as a result of two seismic world wars fought against totalitarian ideologies that assigned *no* importance to the individual. In other words, we cannot help looking today at ancient depictions of human beings of the past and appreciating not only the information we can glean about typical diet, health, height, fashion, gender relations, belief systems, and possible DNA blood lines to ourselves, but also the evidence of an *individual consciousness akin to our own*—a consciousness capable of emotions we still feel today: love, jealousy, fear of death, loyalty, rage, ambition, depression, altruism.

Such curiosity fuels our biographical interest in past figures, and gives us a clue to the second great function of biography in the West—namely, its insight into human character, experience of life, and human emotion, as guides to our own complex *self-understanding,* as individuals.

The Saga of Biography

Before we examine more closely this aspect of biography—its historical key to the secrets that concern us *today* as individuals—let us briefly review the development of life-recording and depiction as they have been practiced over the millennia.

Like all arts and crafts, the practice of depicting and recording individual lives has given rise to a whole series of modalities or tropes, expressed in different ways in different societies, at different times: employing different technologies, from early oral record to the heavily blogged Internet. We cannot, in this brief survey, do justice to those many forms, but by stopping the spool of history at any one point, we can obtain an important archaeological freeze-frame: a glimpse both into a past society via its individuals, and a possible insight into the very *nature of individuality* at any one moment in a culture's history. More, we can appreciate something of the intellectual and artistic means by which "biographers" (though no such word ever existed in the ancient world) were rendering their life portraits—the art and craft of biography, as practiced at certain periods in human history.

For thousands of years, orally recited sagas became and

remained the simplest method of preserving life records, from Homer through the Vinland Saga, from troubadour epics to the *Kalevala*—the latter still being recited to the sounds of the kantele, or zither, in Finland in the mid-nineteenth century, when its widely varying versions were first collected and written down. Easy to memorize via mnemonic techniques—alliteration, repetition, rhyme, rhythm, and characterization—such word-of-mouth retellings answered a variety of social needs, from kinship connection to group entertainment. The extent to which the individuals portrayed in such sagas were real or fictional will always be disputed—but the named characterizations were certainly real enough to the listeners, and important enough for them to survive in infinite variants.

This commemorative-interpretive impulse to record and render individual lives—whether divine, semi-divine, imaginary, realistic, or actual—took a huge leap forward with the invention of writing. For with writing came scripted, *contestable* historical narrative—in *documents*.

Alongside accountancy and diplomacy, written biographical, documentary records—incised in clay, chiseled on stone, painted on papyrus, inked on paper—served to encourage and ensure that significant biographical data, such as the dates and exploits of rulers, would not be lost, or become corrupted by time: information that has proven of enormous help to archaeologists, but also to us as individuals.

The *Epic of Gilgamesh,* recorded in cuneiform on clay tablets in ancient Sumer, is a case in point. Is this poetic life story a fictitious, entertaining narrative about a mythic warrior king, with symbolic lessons for its audience? Or is it also an attempt, within poetic heroic rhetoric, at real-life biography—a literary, poetic memorial to King Gilgamesh, a widely chronicled real ancestor who, as the fifth and most famous monarch of Uruk (the biblical city of Erech, excavated by archaeologists and now the town of Warka, in Iraq), ruled an important city-state in Assyria ca. 2600 B.C.—and thus worthy of ancestor worship?

The story of Gilgamesh's achievements certainly left his Assyrian chroniclers in awe. "In Uruk he built walls, a great rampart, and the temple of the Eanna for the god of the firmament Anu, and Ishtar the goddess of love. Look at it still today," the poets exhorted their audience in the third millennium B.C. "The outer wall where the cornice runs, it shines with the brilliance of copper; and the inner wall, it has no equal. Touch the threshold, it is ancient."

The epic narrative poem was not, however, intended to be a history lesson so much as the *life story,* from youth to death, of a king who had traveled "the countries of the world," was "wise," "saw mysteries," and "knew secret

2. The Flood Tablet of *The Epic of Gilgamesh, King of Ur*—the first literary "biography" ever written, dating back to the second millennium B.C. Written in Akkadian verse and recorded in cuneiform, this version, found in the royal library at Nineveh, dates from the seventh century B.C. *Copyright © Trustees of the British Museum.*

things" gleaned from his "long journey" abroad, "before the flood."

The tale of Gilgamesh's "lust"—a sexual appetite that left "no virgin to her lover, neither the warrior's daughter nor the wife of the noble"—and of his jealousy, struggle, and homoerotic friendship with Enkidu, a man created "like him as his own reflection, his second self, stormy heart for stormy heart," still has the power to move us four thousand years later, whether we think of it as mostly fiction mixed with nonfiction, or vice versa. And it illustrates the eternal questions that hang over biographical portraiture to this very day. *Where does fact end and interpretation begin? Is biography essentially the chronicle of an individual's life journey (and thus a branch of history, employing similar processes of research and scholarship), or is it an art of human portraiture that must, for social and psychologically constructive reasons, capture the essence and distinctiveness of a real individual to be useful both in its time and for posterity?*

Transmission of Personality

Such questions have been asked repeatedly by historians, biographers, writers, artists, and their critics, through the ages. Perhaps it is also the reason that the word "biography"—retro-concocted from the Greek βιος, meaning "life," and γράφ *(graph)*, "depiction"—was not coined in English until the late seventeenth century. It was certainly never used in ancient Greek, and occurred rarely in Latin until the Middle Ages (*biographus, biographia,* denoting written accounts of a life or lives). The very multiplicity and

The Epic of Gilgamesh *is the oldest written biographical story ever found. It details the friendship between the fifth Sumerian king of Uruk (who reigned ca.* 2600 B.C., *and whose probable tomb was discovered in Iraq in* 2003 A.D.*) and his bosom friend Enkidu. Enkidu's death leaves King Gilgamesh distraught:*

When Gilgamesh touched his heart it did not beat. So Gilgamesh laid a veil, as one veils the bride, over his friend. He began to rage like a lion, like a lioness robbed of her whelps. This way and that he paced round the bed, he tore out his hair and strewed it around. He dragged off his splendid robes and flung them down as though they were abominations. . . . The next day also, in the first light, Gilgamesh lamented; seven days and seven nights he wept for Enkidu, until the worm fastened on him. Only then did he give him up to the earth, for the Anunnaki, the judges, had seized him.

Then Gilgamesh issued a proclamation through the land, he summoned them all, the coppersmiths, the goldsmiths, the stone-workers, and commanded them, "Make a statue of my friend." The statue was fashioned with a great weight of lapis lazuli for the breast and gold for the body. A table of hardwood was set out, and on it a bowl of carnelian filled with honey, and a bowl of lapis lazuli filled with butter. These he exposed and offered to the sun; and weeping he went away.

The Epic of Gilgamesh, version by N. K. Sandars, from translations of the Sumerian poem originally on twelve clay tablets dating back before 2000 B.C., with later versions in Akkadian and Hittite (London: Penguin, 1972), pp. 95–96.

diversity of forms and media in which real human beings were depicted, in response to varying agendas and motives, simply ruled out an exclusive generic word such as "biography" that would limit the business either to the oral or written word, or to a specific genre—factual or fictitious.[3]

"Before the dawn of what we call Greek literature," wrote the distinguished historian of classical biography D. R. Stuart, "there were bards who knew how to couch in artistic style the life-histories of warrior princes; there was a public ready to lend its ears to these works of commemoration." Inheriting such traditions, the Greeks had embellished and developed them in myriad forms. "To write the whole story of biographical evolution among the ancients, one must frame a definition broad enough to cover various artistic, verbal records of the deeds, personality, and character of the human unit—records that modern biography," Stuart lamented in 1928, "would not consent to house. Transmission of personality belongs so long a time

---

3. Unknown Egyptian lady, ca. 160 A.D. Reversing thousands of years of stereotyped Egyptian mummy decoration, this stunningly individualistic Hellenistic commemorative portrait was painted in encaustic (pigments mixed with beeswax) on a limewood panel, then buried with the mummy at El Rabayat, in the Fayum region of Egypt. *Copyright © Trustees of the British Museum.*

before Herodotus and Thucydides, Isocrates and Xenophon, that the literary historian, addressing himself to the theme, may well be moved to echo the preface of the harassed Odysseus and inquire: 'What, then, shall I make of my tale? What its end?'"[4]

Nor, we should be clear, was the business of biographical depiction confined to professionals. Every educated Greek or Roman male, for example, would be trained to deliver a eulogy or encomium praising dead figures. Many were taught to paint portraits, sculpt busts, and write about significant people in their lives or the past—what Stuart called "the polymathy of the day."[5] The only "professional" biographer in antique times was the compiler, who put together *collections* of essays about statesmen, soldiers, or philosophers; such collections included Aristoxenus of Tarentum's *Lives of Men,* or Phaenias' *Tyrants of Sicily,* Duris of Samos' *On Painters,* Idomeneus of Lampsacus' *Civic Leaders.*

The educational, even therapeutic moral that emerged from such life studies was felt to be important by both the compiler and the reader. For example, the Roman biographical essayist Plutarch, writing in Greek in the first century A.D., confided (in his *Life of Timoleon*) that he'd begun the "writing of my *Lives* for the sake of others, but now I find that I have grown fond of the task and continue it for my own pleasure. The reason is that it allows me to treat history as a mirror, with the help of which I can adorn my own life by imitating the virtues of the men whose actions I have described. It is as though I could talk with the subjects of my *Lives* and enjoy their company every day, since I receive one in turn, welcome him as my guest, observe with admiration as Priam did of Achilles, '*What was his stature, what his qualities?*' and select from his career those events which are the most important and the most inspiring to record. As Sophocles has written, '*What greater joy could you attain than this?*' And what could do more to raise the standards by which we live?"[6]

In his *Life of Alexander,* Plutarch likened his quest, moreover, to that of a portrait painter, who uses the face and eyes rather than the body to convey the inner man: "In the same way," Plutarch says, prefacing his biographical portrait, "it is my task to dwell upon those actions which illuminate the working of the soul, and by this means to create a portrait of a man's life."[7]

Twin Functions

From the start, then, the twin functions of commemoration, on the one hand, and, on the other, concern with what Edmund Gosse would two millennia later call the "portrait of a soul in its adventures through life,"[8] vied for

4. Thousands of years before the modernist portraits by Pablo Picasso, a double-headed bust of the philosopher Sophocles (left) and the playwright Aristophanes (right) was sculpted in marble to commemorate the two great men, as the golden age of Greek art and biography began. Greece, fourth century B.C. *Copyright © The Louvre, Paris / Bridgeman Art Library.*

biographical expression in almost every art, from poetry to prose, drama to satire, medallions to statuary, painting to jewelry. While formal encomia—for example Isocrates' *Evagoras* of 374 B.C.—became a staple of Greek civilization as expressions of rhetoric and ritualistic commemoration of the dead (the equivalent of obituaries today), public fascination with the details of an individual's life journey spawned an ever-larger number of extraordinary human depictions, exemplified in Xenophon's autobiography *Anabasis* as well as his literary biographies: *Memorabilia* (an essayistic defense of Socrates' life, after the philosopher's execution) and his great *Education of Cyrus,* ca. 350 B.C.

The encomium was expected to drip with didactic praise. "All the hyperboles applied by the poets to men of yore are most appropriate to his nature. If anyone was ever a god among men, Evagoras deserves that title," Isocrates once wrote in an encomium. By contrast, life chronicles opened up the coffins of the dead to more searching present curiosity. From the first lines of his life portrait of Cyrus, for example, the warrior-writer Xenophon sought to ask his reader questions—the better to answer them. How was it, Xenophon asked with intended irony, that, if man is "by nature fitted to govern all creatures, except his fellow men," the Persian leader was able to win for himself "obedience from thousands of his fellows, from cities and tribes innumerable"—even people who "dwelt at a distance which it would take days and months to traverse," including men "who had never set eyes on him, and for the matter of that could never hope to do so, and yet they were willing to obey him"?[9]

Xenophon describes the death of Socrates, in his Memoirs of Socrates, *one of only two contemporary literary portraits of the philosopher, written ca. 380 B.C.:*

It is generally agreed that no one in the memory of man has ever met his death more nobly. He had to live for thirty days after his trial, because the festival of Delos fell in that month, and the law does not permit any publicly sanctioned execution until the mission has returned from Delos. It was evident to his intimate friends that during this time he did not deviate at all from his former way of life—and he had previously been remarkable above all men for the cheerfulness and equanimity of his life. . . . I shall relate also what I heard about him from Hermogenes, the son of

Answering to contemporary curiosity about leadership shown by past figures, Xenophon, as both brave warrior and brilliant autobiographical historian, led the literary way for other chroniclers interested in the study of personality and personal achievement. Plutarch's parallel lives of Alexander the Great and Julius Caesar, written around 100 A.D.,

Hipponicus. He said that, after Meletus had already laid his indictment, he heard Socrates discussing anything rather than the trial and told him that he ought to be considering his defence. At first Socrates said, "Don't you think that my whole life has been a preparation for it?" And when Hermogenes asked him how, he replied that he had spent all his time in studying nothing but questions of right and wrong, doing what was right and refraining from what was wrong; and he considered that this was the finest preparation for defence.

> Xenophon, *Conversations of Socrates*, trans. Hugh Tredennick and Robin Waterfield (Harmondsworth: Penguin, 1990), pp. 214–215.

opened with his now-celebrated explanation of the difference between his own work and that of conventional historians: "It must be borne in mind that my design is not to write histories but lives."

Plutarch's subsequent distinction between the approach of the historian and that of the biographer was wonderfully lucid—indeed, it could easily stand today as a description of the border between the two pursuits. As Plutarch put it, "the most brilliant exploits often tell us nothing of the virtues and vices of the men who performed them," whereas "a chance remark or a joke may reveal far more of a man's character than the mere feat of winning battles in which thousands fall, or marshalling great armies, or laying siege to cities."[10] Siege accounts, he felt, could be "told by others."[11]

Biographical writers such as Plutarch, Suetonius, and Tacitus thus became exceptional among historians for what they *excluded* from historical narrative. They employed the same methods and methodologies as historians (documentary research, interviews, personal memory, background reading), but permitted in their accounts only as much of the "weighty" cultural and social context as would help the audience to better understand their *actual* subject: *the life and character of a distinctive human being.*

Controversial from the Start

Commemoration and *human curiosity:* these two market forces resulted in a demand-led plethora of biographical forms in the classical world, spawning distinctive genres of biographical depiction: from busts of stunning individual realism to portraits on coins; from vivid paintings to extended funeral orations; from epic poetry to bitter satires; from essayistic encomia to scripted dialogues (such as those found on papyrus fragments of Satyrus' brilliant *Life of Euripides,* dating back to the third century B.C.); from oral sagas and recited lineages to whole compendia of famous lives, such as those compiled by historians and writers like Philostratus, Eunapius, Cornelius Nepos, Suetonius, Marius Maximus, and others (most of which, like broken sculptures, survive only in fragments). Nor was ancient biography confined to the record of *others.* The biography of oneself (idiography—or "autobiography," as it later came to be known) was from the start an intrinsic part of human society's self-recording: biographical and autobiographical accounts acting together as mutually corrective interpretations of individual lives. Every work of biography or autobiography had, after all, its agenda, conscious or unconscious, laudatory or critical, whether recording an individual's actions or his reflections. Seen in retrospect, both perspectives—biographies of others and memoirs in classical times—thus displayed, from the start, an abiding tension between commemoration and critical interpretation—memoirs offering their authors the opportunity for egotistical or self-gratifying self-depiction, but also a greater potential for a more thoughtful focus on the internal as well as external life of its author—as Seneca showed in his

Letters from a Stoic (ca. 65 A.D.) or Emperor Marcus Aurelius in his Stoic reflections, *To Myself* (171–180 A.D.).

This extended period of biographical development was biography's first "golden age": a wealth of knowledge and Greek real-life descriptive art to which Roman biographers added their own, less philosophical yet more practical skills and their obsession with method, accuracy, gossip, and historical evidence.

Ego played an important part in this. Julius Caesar for example, proud of his accomplishments, famously issued coins bearing his own likeness, posed for many a statue, and even recorded his own military triumphs in his *Gallic Wars* (51 A.D.). His driving force was his ambition, but his more reflective concern was to enhance his own reputation as a leader and general. Moreover, such self-advertising, as with aspiring political leaders today, did him no harm. Not only was he able to acquire the beautiful young Cleopatra as his mistress, but, after his extraordinary victories in battle, he became *dictator perpetuus* in Rome.

Yet what kind of man *was* Caesar, really? How self-serving was his own version of events? His memoirs gave little idea—and, de facto, could not relate the last great event of his life: his brutal murder by his compatriots. For that, biographies were necessary, and contemporary biographers were only too pleased to oblige. To make other men's lives accessible, and their life journeys convincing, it became important to include "telling detail." Of Julius Caesar's appearance, for example, Suetonius noted: "His baldness was a disfigurement which his enemies harped upon, much to his exasperation; but he used to comb the thin strands of hair forward from his poll, and of all the honors voted him by the Senate and the People, none pleased him so much as the privilege of wearing a laurel wreath on all occasions—he constantly took advantage of it." This observation could have been made two millennia later of the British general Field Marshal Montgomery, who was uniquely authorized by the king to wear two distinctive badges on his black beret—headgear that not only made him more distinctive on the battlefield, but conveniently covered his balding, less distinguished pate. Similarly, Caesar's dress code was deliberately casual, like Churchill's famous blue boiler-suit thousands of years later. "His dress was, it seems, unusual," Hadrian's secretary noted of Julius Caesar, for "he had added wrist-length sleeves with fringes to his purple-striped senatorial tunic, and the belt which he wore over it was never fastened." Hence Sulla's warning to the aristocratic party: "Beware of that boy with the loose clothes."[12]

Through such individualized characterization the reader could, like someone viewing a portrait, see into the life of

———oᴙᴙo———

Suetonius' account (ca. 110 A.D.) of the death of the Roman
tyrant Nero:

Finally, when his companions unanimously insisted on
his trying to escape from the degrading fate threatening him, he ordered them to dig a grave at once, of
the right size, and then collect any pieces of marble
that they could find and fetch wood and water for the
disposal of the corpse. As they bustled about obedi-
ently he muttered through his tears: "Dead! And so
great an artist!"

While he hesitated, a runner brought him a letter
from Phaon. Nero tore it from the man's hands and
read that, having been declared a public enemy by the
Senate, he would be punished "in ancient style" when
arrested. He asked what "ancient style" meant, and
learned that the executioners stripped their victim naked, thrust his head into a wooden fork, and then

flogged him to death with rods. In terror he snatched up the two daggers which he had brought along and tried their points; but threw them down again, protesting that the fatal hour had not yet come. Then he begged Sporus to weep and mourn for him, but also begged one of the other three to set him an example by committing suicide first. He kept moaning about his cowardice, and muttering: "How ugly and vulgar my life has become!" And then in Greek: "This is certainly no credit to Nero, no credit at all," and: "Come, pull yourself together!" By this time the troop of cavalry who had orders to take him alive were coming up the road. Nero gasped: *"Hark to the sound I hear! It is hooves of galloping horses."*

Suetonius, "Nero," in *The Twelve Caesars,* trans. Robert Graves, ed. Michael Grant (London: Allen Lane, 1979), p. 206.

a recognizable fellow human being rather than that of an enlarged, deified, or mythic figure for whom one might feel awe but limited identification.

This golden, classical age of life depiction, we should note, was characterized by the same fundamental tension seen today, straining at the biographical core, beyond simple, factual information. The motives for life depiction had, in an age of aqueducts, highways, grand architecture, competitive sports, high rhetoric, and empire, become enormously varied: expressing and responding to multiple needs, from documentation to entertainment, and in a plethora of media, from sculpted busts to stelae, library books to wall paintings, humorous skits to great monuments. At their center, though, the age-old tug of war between idealization and critical interpretation still characterized the biographical enterprise. Some Romans wanted to laud and worship ancestors and past figures, the better to establish or reinforce their own identity. Others found that this idealization could not square with their curiosity to know more about the psychology and *real* life experiences of an unidealized individual, the better to understand their own lives. It was this tension that marked biography from its beginnings—and marks it still, today.

ℋagiography

$\mathcal{C}$ ommemoration versus critical depiction: this was a biographical rift that would never go away. Indeed, we all know, in the recent past, the story of Clementine Churchill's decision to destroy the brilliantly modern but unflattering portrait of her husband, Sir Winston Churchill, which loyal members of Parliament had commissioned from Graham Sutherland following World War II.

Such an outraged response to biographical portraiture by an aggrieved family member who is hurt in her idealized identity (living as an adjunct to greatness) has been common for thousands of years. Biography is, in this sense, not simply human record but debate—debate that goes back to biography's first golden age, as when Plutarch excoriated Herodotus for misrepresentation of individuals in order to concoct neat historical plots, and to Suetonius and Tacitus, who reveled in stripping the masks from much-commemorated heroes of Greece and Rome.

With the collapse of the Roman Empire, however, the first golden age of biography came to an end. Life depiction reverted to its largely commemorative role in European tribal society—a development that was compounded by the rise of Christianity.

The Hebrew Scriptures, also known as the Old Testament, Old Covenant, Septuagint (so named for the seventy elders of Israel who translated the scriptures into Greek at Alexandria), or Jewish Bible, had evolved in many forms as a biographical compendium of the ancient Jewish world, dating back to the time of Solomon and David. The Scriptures were based not only on songs, oral legend, traditions, and court records, but increasingly on the scripted histo-

---

5. Early Orthodox Jewish rules forbade the graphic representation of divine or human figures in biblical work. Yet the abundance of extraordinary human stories related in the Torah made it almost impossible not to illustrate people, especially in competition with Christian art. Shown here is a page from Maimonides' *Mishneh Torah,* or record of Jewish law, inked on vellum ca. 1381. *Copyright ©* *National Library, Jerusalem / Bridgeman Art Library.*

ries (recorded on papyrus rolls or vellum) of the tribes of Israel—mixing more than a thousand years of speculative and documented genealogy, encomia, rhetoric, poetry, prophecy, and love of narrative, in memorable depictions (from a variety of sources) of individual men and women, heroes and villains: Adam and Eve, Cain and Abel, Aaron and Abigail, Absalom and Ahab, Amos and Abraham, Bathsheba and Bilhah, Daniel and David, Dinah and Delilah, Elijah and Esau, Isaiah, Isaac, Jacob, Joseph, Job, Jeremiah, Jonah, Jezebel, Jeroboam, Moses, Noah, Saul, Sampson and Solomon, Rachel and Sarah, Ruth, Sheba and Tamar, Tobit and Uriah.

Yet it was the singular, scripted life story of one particular Jew, Jesus of Nazareth, as written by four biographical authors at the end of the first century A.D., that marked a wholly new, symbolic power in Western life depiction.

Fundamentalist Christians might later hold to a line of divine "inerrancy"—that no statement in the "Bible" could ever be untrue, however many authors there had been, or however variant their collected papyrus rolls and vellum books in Aramaic, Hebrew, Greek, Latin, or English translation might be. But this fundamentalist view of the Bible as the incontestable "word of God" overlooked the triumph of the four Gospels of the New Testament *as biogra-*

phy. The fact was, the Old Testament had been a pageant. The New Testament was a one-star show.

Authorized Biography

The "Good News" delineation of Jesus of Nazareth's life overrode all previous encomia. Chronicling the background to Jesus' birth, his miraculous conception, his delivery in a simple manger, his upbringing, disappearance, temptation by Satan, ministry, struggle with authority, arrest, interrogation, trial, and death by public execution, as well as his resurrection and afterlife, it was indeed the "greatest story ever told"—for the four chosen biographies, or Gospels, demonstrated what P. M. Kendall, in a look at the art of written biography, once described as "great originality"[1]—that "by their homely detail, their use of anecdote and dialogue, their emphasis on feeling, their depiction of personality in crisis, they thrust us into the living texture of a life."[2]

Interestingly, it is often forgotten that Plutarch, Suetonius, and Tacitus (whose *Agricola* was a monumental work of serious biographical chronicling) were Greco-Roman contemporaries of Mark, Matthew, Luke, and John, and by no means lesser biographers—indeed, they were far better *historians* in terms of research and documentation. How-

---

The Gospel According to Mark, recording the indictment and condemnation of Jesus:

And they led Jesus to the high priest; and all the chief priests and the elders were assembled. And Peter had followed him at a distance, right into the courtyard of the high priest; and he was sitting with the guards, and warming himself at the fire. Now the chief priests and the whole council sought testimony against Jesus to put him to death; but they found none. For many bore false witness against him, and their witness did not agree. . . . And the high priest stood up in the midst, and asked Jesus, "Have you no answer to make? What is it that these men testify against you?" But he was silent and made no answer. Again the high priest asked

---

ever, the mythic power of the Jesus story, as divine encomium in four-part harmony, simply elbowed other biographers off the Middle Eastern and Western stages.

Determined to copyright such a brilliant and *evocative* biography, Christian leaders soon rounded on competing versions of Christ's biography and condemned them as

him, "Are you the Christ, the Son, of the Blessed?"
And Jesus said, "I am; and you will see the Son of man
sitting at the right hand of Power, and coming with
the clouds of heaven." And the high priest tore his
mantle, and said, "Why do we still need witnesses?
You have heard his blasphemy. What is your decision?"
And they all condemned him as deserving death. And
some began to spit on him, and to cover his face, and
to strike him, saying to him, "Prophesy!" And the
guards received him with blows.

> The Gospel According to Mark—commonly thought to
> have been the first written of the authorized four Gos-
> pels—in *The Oxford Annotated Bible, with Apocrypha*, Re-
> vised Standard Version (Oxford: Oxford University Press),
> 14:53–65.

heretical. Alternative, less deifying, and literally death-
defying biographies by writers such as the Gnostic chronicler Thomas were damned, destroyed, or driven into con-
cealment by the early Christian church authorities for
almost two thousand years.[3]

With biographical competition removed, then, the sim-

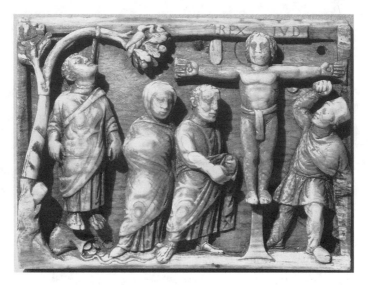

6. Recorded in every art form, the life and death of Jesus of Nazareth swiftly became the most popular human story in the Middle Eastern and Western worlds. This is the oldest known illustration of Christ on the Cross, flanked by his mother, Mary, and John the Evangelist, carved ca. 400 A.D. on ivory, probably for a Communion-bread holder. *Copyright © Trustees of the British Museum / Bridgeman Art Library.*

plified collection or monopoly, comprising four reasonably similar gospel stories, became the authorized version of Jesus' life—the mainstay of the New Testament. The Bible, as a result, was freed to become the best-selling biographical work of all time.

The Dark Ages

Would the Christian biography of Jesus have maintained such best-selling status without the collapse of Roman civilization? Perhaps—though as a more vivid, populist biography in competition with the more scholarly works of Plutarch, Suetonius, Tacitus, and others.

It was not to be, however. Following the fall of Rome, illiteracy and tribal anarchy—the so-called Dark Ages—swept through the Western world. Greco-Roman culture was for the most part abandoned while, in a return to earlier, Homeric times, biographical depiction reverted to communal, word-of-mouth storytelling. Viking sagas, for instance, repeated the sequential cycle of first oral, then printed or decorative biographical record and interpretation of the Vikings' own heroes, ancestors, enemies, and others.

Gradually, however, even the Vikings were converted to Christianity. The quadragraphic Jesus biography, with its stories of miracles, pain, and redemption, proved all-conquering. Moreover, stories of apostles, martyrs, and saints, reverently embellished, added further luster to the Christian epic—especially when Saint Augustine penned his own biography, or autobiography.

The Gnostic Gospel according to Mary Magdalene (second century A.D.; considered too feminist, and therefore heretical), describes in Chapter 9 her conversation with the risen Christ—and the skepticism of the male disciples:

When Mary had said this, she fell silent, since it was to this point that the Savior had spoken with her.

But Andrew answered and said to the brethren: Say what you wish to say about what she has said. I at least do not believe that the Savior said this. For certainly these teachings are strange ideas.

Peter answered and spoke concerning these same things.

He questioned them about the Savior: Did He really speak privately with a woman and not openly to us? Are we to turn about and all listen to her? Did He prefer her to us?

Then Mary wept and said to Peter: My brother Peter, what do you think? Do you think that I have thought this up myself in my heart, or that I am lying about the Savior?

Levi answered and said to Peter: Peter you have always been hot-tempered.

Now I see you contending against the woman like the adversaries.

But if the Savior made her worthy, who are you indeed to reject her? Surely the Savior knows her very well.

That is why He loved her more than us. Rather, let us be ashamed and put on the perfect Man, and separate as He commanded us and preach the gospel, not laying down any other rule or other law beyond what the Savior said.

And when they heard this, they began to go forth to proclaim and to preach.

The Gospel According to Mary Magdalene, text from the *Akhmim Codex (Papyrus Berolinensis 8502)*—remnant of a Coptic codex acquired in Cairo in 1896 by a German scholar, Dr. Carl Reinhardt. Gnostic Society Library, at www.webcom.com/gnosis/library/marygosp.htm. See Elaine Pagels, *The Gnostic Gospels* (New York: Vintage, 1979), pp. 64–65. A further gospel, or codex, namely that of Judas Iscariot, was pieced together, transcribed, and translated from fragments also found in Egypt, in 2006.

Saint Augustine's Confessions

Many Greeks and Romans, from Xenophon to Julius Caesar, had penned their memoirs—but these idiographies, in a virtually illiterate Europe, were almost entirely forgotten. Saint Augustine's stunning *Confessions,* by contrast, written early in the fifth century A.D., struck deeper to the heart of the human self, as the basis of biography, than ever before or after—indeed, they have remained in print ever since.[4]

Exploring the tension between selfishness and self-sacrifice, Augustine—who had converted to Christianity in 387 A.D. and was determined to tell God the absolute truth about himself—allowed fellow Christians to listen in. "I went to Carthage," he says in the chronicle of his sexual life journey, "where I found myself in the midst of a hissing cauldron of lust." Nor did he balk at describing his own weakness for sex. "To love and to have my love returned was my heart's desire, and it would be all the sweeter if I could also enjoy the body of the one who loved me. So I muddied the stream of friendship with the filth of lewdness and clouded its clear waters with hell's black river of lust." He fell in love, his love was returned, he had sex with his girlfriend. "In the midst of my joy, he noted, "I was caught up in the coils of trouble, for I was lashed with the cruel, fiery rods of jealousy and suspicion, fear, anger, and quarrels."[5]

Not even the life of the much-married prophet Mohammed and the assembling of the Koran could or would later match the sheer *biographical* intensity of Saint Augustine's confessions and the Jesus story. Moreover, the *marketing* of such biographies was impeccable—indeed the Bible, Peter Calvocoressi has written, "is the most widely disseminated book in the world. The root cause of this phenomenon is the demand for the Christian scriptures, reinforced by missionary zeal and a degree of *gratis* distribution unparalleled before the deluge of modern advertising."[6]

Yet marketing alone could not maintain the Bible's status as the best-read book in the West, as Calvocoressi knew—indeed, so impressed was he by "the Book" that he personally compiled a *Who's Who in the Bible,* recognizing that it was not simply the story of Jesus and his contemporaries that fascinated readers, but a veritable *biographical gallery* of earlier figures of religious, political, and social history, exemplified in Old Testament prophets—Isaiah, Jeremiah, Ezekiel, Amos, Hosea, Micah, Deutero-Isaiah, and others.

Armed with this traveling biographical archive, so to

Saint Augustine's autobiographical confession (ca. 397), addressed to God:

Meanwhile I was sinning more and more. The woman with whom I had been living was torn from my side as an obstacle to my [arranged] marriage, and this was a blow which crushed my heart to bleeding, because I loved her dearly. She went back to Africa, vowing never to give herself to any other man, and left with me the son whom she had borne me. But I was too unhappy and too weak to imitate this example set me by a woman. I was impatient at the delay of two years which had to pass before the girl I had asked to marry became my wife, and because I was more a slave of

speak, priests, monks, friars, and nuns spread their biblical life stories across the Christian-contested world—with Saint Augustine's *Confessions* a welcome, modern autobiographical addition. Moreover, as the centuries passed, there were further biographical and autobiographical additions to the Christian library—additions which we know today under their collective name: hagiography.

lust than a true lover of marriage, I took another mistress, without the sanction of wedlock. This meant that the disease of my soul would continue unabated, in fact it would be aggravated, and under the watch and ward of uninterrupted habit it would persist into the state of marriage. Furthermore, the wound that I had received when my first mistress was wrenched away showed no sign of healing. At first the pain was sharp and searing, but then the wound began to fester, and though the pain was duller there was also less hope of a cure.

Saint Augustine of Hippo, *Confessions,* trans. R. S. Pine-Coffin (Harmondsworth: Penguin, 1961), p. 131.

Tens, hundreds, and eventually thousands of new names would be added to the Christian biographical canon: the life stories of Christian adherents and their adventures and misadventures as they sought to spread the Good News, either in defiance of an outside, unenlightened world, or in struggle with their own baser, sinful, personal selves.

Thus, the great biblical biographical narratives of Judaism gave rise to, and were complemented by, the Christian epic and its concomitants. Moreover, this development was not confined to written biographies. In a Western world in which literacy was confined to a tiny percentage of the population, graphic representation was as powerful as the scriptural saga—indeed, often more so. Jesus' nativity, miracles, trial, crucifixion, and companions were depicted, redepicted, and endlessly reinterpreted in what later became known as Christian art—but which was, to the people of Europe, the word, image, and working of God.

Christianized Biography

The Greco-Roman golden age of biography, then, vanished with its empires, replaced by childlike, yet powerful biographical idealizations illuminating a Dark Ages of almost universal philistinism.

Without Christianity and Christian biography, would illiterate Europe have succumbed after the sixth century to its rival, Islam—a religion that eschewed individual life depiction as insulting to the majesty of Allah? If so, we can be sure it would have spelled the end of biography—even if that biography had become, for the moment, largely hagiography.

We do not have the time here to analyze in detail the Christian contribution to biography—both positive and negative. But it is worth noting how much it deepened the focus upon the individual *self.* In Islam, the graphic depiction of individual mortals was forbidden. In Hindu civilization, the world's oldest organized religion, the individual self likewise had, in practice, virtually no importance, since the human soul (Atman) is best united with the ultimate truth (Brahman) through contemplation and meditation, not deed. According to the doctrine of Karma, the cumulative effects of a person's actions ought to have great importance—yet in actuality they have little, owing to the *transmigration of the soul,* in which one's soul moves after death into another body, producing a continuing cycle of birth, life, death, and rebirth through many lifetimes: *samsara.* The depiction of an individual in the midst of this transmigrating trail is thus considered too transitory and unimportant to others to be worth recording—just as the unequal distribution of wealth, prestige, and suffering is accepted as a natural consequence of people's previous, but unrecorded, acts in earlier, unknown lives.

Christian belief, by contrast, concentrated upon personal salvation in *this* life, and the avoidance of hell in the next, by following the example of Jesus as described by his four authorized biographers: an agenda that made Christian biography central to European culture, once Christianity prevailed.

Adamnan's biography (ca. 690 A.D.) of Saint Columba, Chapter 16, "Regarding a Certain Unhappy Man Who Lay with His Mother":

At another time, the saint called out the brethren at the dead of night, and when they were assembled in the church said to them: "Now let us pray fervently to the Lord, for at this hour a sin unheard of in the world has been committed, for which rigorous vengeance that is justly due is very much to be feared." Next day he spoke of this sin to a few who were asking him about it. "After a few months," he said, "that unhappy wretch will come here to the Iouan island [Hy, now Iona] with Lugaid, who is unaware of the sin." Accordingly, after the few months had passed away, the saint one day spoke to Diormit, and ordered him, "Rise quickly; lo! Lugaid is coming. Tell him to send off the wretch whom he has with him in the ship to the Malean island [Mull], that he may not tread the sod of this island." He went to the sea in obedience to the saint's injunction, and told Lugaid as he was approaching all the words of the saint regarding the unhappy man. On hearing the directions, that unhappy man vowed that he would never eat food with others until he had seen Saint Columba and spoken to him. Diormit therefore returned to the saint, and told him the words of the poor wretch. The saint, on hearing them, went down to the haven, and as Baitan was citing the authority of Holy Scriptures, and suggesting that the repentance of the unhappy man should be received, the saint immediately replied to him, "O Baitan! this man has committed fratricide like Cain, and become an adulterer with his mother." Then the poor wretch, casting himself upon his knees on the beach, promised that he would comply with all the rules of penance, according to the judgment of the saint. The saint said to him, "If thou do penance in tears and lamentations for twelve years among the Britons and never to the day of thy death return to Scotia [Ireland], perhaps God may pardon thy sin." Having said these words, the saint turned to his own friends and said, "This man is a son of perdition, who will not perform the penance he has promised, but will soon return to Scotia, and there in a short time be killed by his enemies." All this happened exactly according to the saint's prophecy; for the wretched man, returning to Hibernia about the same time, fell into the hands of his enemies in the region called Lea [Firli, in Ulster], and was murdered. He was of the descendants of Turtre.

Life of Saint Columba, Founder of Hy; Written by Adamnan, Ninth Abbot of That Monastery, ed. William Reeves (Edinburgh: Edmonston and Douglas, 1874).

7. Hagiography, or the lives of saints, dominated all the biographical arts throughout the Middle Ages and beyond. The saints were usually portrayed in the context of the artists' own times. Here, Albrecht Dürer's 1514 engraving of Saint Jerome (331–420 A.D., re-translator of the Bible from Hebrew and Greek into popular Latin, a version known as the Vulgate) depicts the literary saint working in his study. In the foreground is the lion from whose paw he was reputed to have removed a thorn. *Copyright © Bibliothèque Nationale, Paris / Bridgeman Art Library.*

Saying No to Voluptuous Imagination

The downside of such Christian focus on the individual, biographically speaking, was to be found in the Christian laundry—from which life depictions emerged whitened and clean, as moral exemplars to others.

Such moral—and moralizing—teaching was, of course, not new. Had not Marcus Aurelius, for instance, extolled in his Roman autobiography clean living and clean *thinking,* so that "if a man upon a sudden should ask thee, what it is that thou art now thinking, thou mayest answer This and That, freely and boldly, that so by thy thoughts it may presently appear that all in thee is sincere and peaceable: as becometh one that is made for society, and regards not pleasure, nor gives way to voluptuous imaginations at all."

Voluptuous imaginations became *streng verboten,* at least in sanitized Christian literature. Since the emphasis of Christian faith was on personal quest and salvation through the defeat of temptation and sin, Christian biography should in principle have maintained a personal spotlight on the sin-tested torment of the individual. As in India, it all too often didn't—for the Catholic church, as an institution, came to control biography, in both literary production and graphic imagery, eventually issuing an *Index librorum prohibitorum* (list of forbidden books), policed by the Inquisition. By continually extolling and romanticizing the official, idealized biography of Jesus and the Saints, the Christian church thus encouraged ethically pure biography and religious belief, in a search for orthodoxy of veneration—while in their real lives the majority of Christians behaved with the utmost arrogance, especially toward nonbelievers.

A Pass to the Celestial Kingdom

Assyrian biographers of Gilgamesh, three millennia before, had extolled a king who had been willing to travel and learn about the world beyond his palace and city. A major problem with the Christianization of biography was, as Hugh Whittemore has pointed out, not only its propensity to "launder" life stories but also its complacency. Willfully ignorant of the glories of Greco-Roman culture, Christian biographers extolled, for example, the life of Saint Anthony—his chronicler Athanasius pointing to the fatuousness of broadening one's horizons and knowledge in achieving virtue. "Greeks," he sneered, "go abroad and cross the sea and study letters, but we have no need to go abroad for the Kingdom of Heaven, nor to cross the sea to obtain virtue. The Lord has told us in advance the Kingdom of Heaven is within us."[7]

Save in briefly mentioning the vices that the saintly

Christian heroes were meeting and rejecting, church-sponsored hagiography sidelined the potential of secular biography to increase human knowledge and understanding through the depiction of less-than-saintly, unlaundered lives. In the shadow of Saint Augustine's intimate *Confessions,* authorized hagiographers largely confined themselves to stories of the attainment of goodness, and the earning of a pass to the celestial kingdom. To their credit however, as Whittemore allowed, Christian biographical writers and artists did introduce to the biographical canon the lives of *ordinary,* humble believers—especially women—rather than adhering to the exclusive community of statesmen, soldiers, poets, and philosophers of the Greco-Roman golden age of biography. Furthermore, Christian autobiography, inspired by Saint Augustine, took the more reflective, life-contemplative approach to the human self to new heights—indeed, this revolutionary approach to autobiography allowed the humblest, most unsuccessful memoirist, even a woman such as the fifteenth-century Margery of Kempe, to explore and relate personal adventures in the "real" world—the world of the soul.[8]

A Key to the Self

What fascinates the historian of biography about this morally reflective, increasingly confessional arena (once Christians had constructed the pyramid of sin) is the dialectic of biography: namely, the way autobiographers were able to apply a creative whip to the flanks of stoic (but not Stoic) biographers: *daring,* as autobiographers, to look into areas of the self denied to biographers, who could not know (save from reading such accounts, or getting such sources to talk about their inner lives) what was going on in the minds of the individuals they depicted.

Biography, largely as a result of Christianity, thus became a record of the individual human *mind* as much as of the exploits of a person. Christian and post-Christian self-depicters thereby became the most self-challenging of biographers—licensed by the example of Saint Augustine's candor to move outside the biographical, third-party descriptive mode to prod, investigate, question, and openly debate in the present, current, still-living tense. Biographers, as chroniclers for the most part of past lives in a church-policed culture of veneration, were unable to do this.

Ironically, the Christian church had with one hand constrained the once-glorious richness of Roman biographers, in the drive to maintain Christian cohesion and religious dominance in Europe, through regulated piety. Yet with the other it also opened up, through autobiographers, a rich new confessional dialogue with God that readers could

eavesdrop on. In his *Confessions,* the sincere, painfully honest Saint Augustine had permitted himself to be emotional—which in a biographer would immediately have di-
minished his objectivity in the eyes of a reader—because
he was addressing his confession directly to God, not to
the church. Spellbound, his audience was thus enabled, as
if through a secretly planted microphone, to listen in on
one of the greatest self-depictions in history, as Augustine
bared his sins, his torments, and his soul. "I had grown
up and grown more vicious with the years," Augustine
confided to his Maker in charting his conversion to Christianity from Manichaeism. "I was a fool who laughed at
the cure you prescribed when you saved me, in my state of
sin, from twofold death, the death of the body and the
death of the soul."[9]

Augustine's confessional dialogue with the God of
Christianity has marked the development of autobiography to this day—not only compelling, by its example, reflective autobiographers (i.e., those writers and artists
seeking to go beyond simple memoir) to try to be radically
truthful in the record of their actions, but also challenging
and depicting their inner, self-conscious selves. By the attention they paid to the ethical choices available to each individual human being, Christian autobiographers focused
upon the life story of the individual as a drama of the

moral self—a focus that would remain long after the secularization of the Western world.

It was this dramatic *self*, however, that was bound to break out from its Christianized *blanchisserie* once literacy increased, printing was invented, and prosperity empowered ordinary as well as extraordinary people to gain access to *knowledge*. With the new dawn of the Renaissance, church-maintained biographical barriers began to lift in the West, and fresh life blew into both the fictional and the nonfictional representations of human beings. The result would be the secularization of learning—leading out of hagiography into modern biography.

CHAPTER 3

The Renaissance of Biography

The power of religious authorities to contain life depiction within set parameters continues to this day in a variety of nations—most notably Islamic countries. The rise of the secular state in Europe, however, and what Jacob Burckhardt, in his *Civilization of the Renaissance in Italy,* called "the development of the individual," changed the face and fate of Western history—and biography. Hitherto man had been, according to Burckhardt, "conscious of himself only as a member of a race, people, party, family or corporation." With the onset of the Renaissance he became a "spiritual *individual* and recognized himself as such."[1]

Not only did Western man become cognizant of his individuality—he unleashed his own curiosity: about himself and about others. From the Renaissance onward, Western biographical depictions showed a return to the classical struggle between, on the one hand, the commemoration of the dead as a continuing spur to more moral behavior by the living, and, on the other, the need to be able to identify with the trials and tribulations of another mortal individual's life journey, as an aid to modern self-understanding, even self-acceptance.

It was in this reflowering of Western civilization that historians and artists switched their attention from the hagiographic portraits of saints and began depicting *secular* individuals on a scale and with a passion reminiscent of classical times.

Plutarch's *Lives of the Noble Grecians and Romans* were now translated and republished. Duris of Samos' *On Painters* was the inspiration for new works such as Giorgio Vasari's great *Lives of the Artists,* while the autobiography of virtuoso goldsmith Benvenuto Cellini took over from Isocrates' *Antidosus,* the point at which self-depiction had begun. Portrait painting, thanks to the economic boom

Benvenuto Cellini wrote his celebrated autobiography in the years 1558–1566. Here the master goldsmith relates some of the (exaggerated) adventures in his self-styled "troubled career":

The plague went dragging on for many months, but I had as yet managed to keep it at bay; for though several of my comrades were dead, I survived in health and freedom. Now it chanced one evening that an intimate comrade of mine brought home to supper a Bolognese prostitute named Faustina. She was a very fine woman, but about thirty years of age; and she had with her a little serving-girl of thirteen or fourteen. Faustina belonging to my friend, I would not have touched her for all the gold in the world; and though she declared she was madly in love with me, I remained steadfast in my loyalty. But after they had gone to bed, I stole away the little serving-girl, who was quite a fresh maid, and woe to her if her mistress had known of it! The result was that I enjoyed a very pleasant night, far more to my satisfaction than if I had passed it with Faustina. I rose upon the hour of breaking fast, and felt tired, for I had travelled many miles that night, and was wanting to take food, when a crushing headache seized me; several boils appeared on my left arm, together with a carbuncle which showed itself just beyond the palm of the left hand where it joins the wrist. Everybody in the house was in a panic; my friend, the cow, and the calf all fled. Left alone there with my poor little prentice, who refused to abandon me, I felt stifled at the heart, and made up my mind for certain I was a dead man.

Just then the father of the lad went by, who was physician to the Cardinal Iacoacci, and lived as member of that prelate's household. The boy called out: "Come, father, and see Benvenuto; he is in bed with some trifling indisposition." Without thinking what my complaint might be, the doctor came up at once, and when he had felt my pulse, he saw and felt what was very contrary to his own wishes. Turning round to his son, he said: "O traitor of a child, you've ruined me; how can I venture now into the Cardinal's presence?" His son made answer: "Why, father, this man my master is worth far more than all the cardinals in Rome." Then the doctor turned to me and said:

"Since I am here, I will consent to treat you. But of one thing only I warn you, that if you have enjoyed a woman, you are doomed." To this I replied: "I did so this very night." He answered: "With whom, and to what extent?" I said: "Last night, and with a girl in her earliest maturity." Upon this, perceiving that he had spoken foolishly, he made haste to add: "Well, considering the sores are so new, and have not yet begun to stink, and that the remedies will be taken in time, you need not be too much afraid, for I have good hopes of curing you."

The Autobiography of Benvenuto Cellini, trans. John Addington Symonds (New York: P. F. Collier, 1910), ch. 29.

in Europe, proliferated anew, and in England, Raphael Holinshed produced his three-million-word historical compendium of English, Irish, and Scottish lives—which in turn fueled as many as twelve of William Shakespeare's historical-biographical plays.

Biography was approaching its second golden age.

The relationship between Holinshed and Shakespeare introduces a new element to our biographical overview:

namely, the *dramatization* of real-life stories—an element that has become even more pertinent today, in an obsessively "reality-TV" age where the dramatic rights to every major real-life human news story are sought immediately.

The story of Jesus of Nazareth had, of course, been recorded, interpreted, and dramatized in a wide cross-section of media, from statuary to mosaics, crucifixes to medallions, paintings to tapestries, processions to plainsong, oratorios to Passion plays. What the Renaissance now added was a larger and more educated market for *secular* lives to be equally commemorated—and interpreted. This William Shakespeare did with such magical dramatic skill that, as with the Gospel authors Mark, Matthew, Luke, and John, Shakespeare's history plays would mold public perception of his chosen kings and queens of England ever afterward—to the point where their life stories are seen not only as biographies or even dramatizations of biographies, but as the world's greatest creative literature.

What, then, *is* the relationship between biography and literature, we ask ourselves?

Over the years, many biographers as well as literary critics and writers have puzzled over this question—in particular, Virginia Woolf, whose father, Leslie Stephen, was a professional biographical compiler. We shall certainly not be able to offer a definitive answer here. Nevertheless, we might make some observations which may help clarify the topic.

After centuries of church-sponsored ignorance, curiosity about secular figures of the past became epidemic in Europe—a ready market for Shakespeare's dramatizations of nonreligious lives (he never did write about a saint).[2] Moreover, whereas nonfiction prose writers felt constrained by the straitjacket of historical, antiquarian scholarship, the Bard felt licensed to speculate and interpret at will— looking into the "empty corners" of history, where angels and scholars feared to tread, in order to explore the secrets of psychologically realistic, as opposed to idealized, leadership and decision making.

In Shakespeare's comedies love's illusions, inanities, cuckoldries, and delights were paraded; in his tragedies, adultery, jealousy, murder, and suicide were relentlessly explored through fictional and nonfictional life stories. No biographical historian had tested the mythology of supposedly real lives in such a way since classical times (when skeptical minds such as Aristoxenus had, for example, contested the idealized view of Socrates, maintaining that the philosopher was sensual, selfish, ignorant, temperamental, and a bigot). The result, in the case of Shakespeare, was a new miracle of creative stage drama and language—as well as psychological insight and biographical characterization, however factually incorrect or mythic.

Dangerous Lives

Shakespeare's influence on biographical depiction would be revolutionary: in particular, his indelible case studies of leader figures, such as Richard II and even Hamlet, who are psychologically unable to bear the burdens of leadership and expectation. This was a life lesson any playgoer could relate to, without wearing the vestments of a king.

That the lesson was immediately learned in Tudor Britain not by biographical chroniclers, but only by dramatists, was due in part to the heavy hand of antiquarian historiography—and the state of the union.

Let us take the latter first. The nearer Shakespeare came to his own day in his historical-biographical dramatizations, the more careful he had to be to avoid the wrath of the powerful: the monarch or senior court officials, protector-patrons of the arts—and the Lord Chamberlain, or stage censor. Which brings us back to the problem that has haunted biography as perhaps no other art or practice: subversive biography—especially about living people.

The case of Shakespeare's contemporary Sir Walter

THE

HISTORIE OF

THE VVORLD.

IN FIVE BOOKES.

1   Ntreating of the *Beginning and first Ages of the same from the Creation vnto* Abraham.
2   Of the *Times from the Birth of* Abraham, *to the destruction of the Temple of* Salomon.
3   From the destruction of Ierusalem, to the time of Philip of Macedon.
4   From the Reigne of Philip of Macedon, to the establishing of that Kingdome, in the Race of Antigonus.
5   From the settled rule of Alexanders successours in the East, vntill the Romans (prevailing over all) made Conquest of Asia and Macedon.

By Sir WALTER RALEGH, Knight.

VERA EFFIGIES CLARISSIMI VIRI DOMINI GUALTHERI RALEGH EQV. AUR. etc.

The true and lively portraiture of the honourable and learned Knight Sr. Walter Ralegh.

MORE DAVERE

Raleigh—soldier, seaman, geographer, philosopher, poet, historian, courtier—provides us, in this respect, with the saddest example of biography's tightrope walk. Raleigh's farcical trial in 1603 (on the charge of being a Spanish spy) had produced a considerable outcry, causing the new monarch of the union between Scotland and England, King James I, to rescind the order for Raleigh's execution and instead order the poet conveyed to the Tower of London "at his Majesty's pleasure." There, Raleigh languished for more than a decade, scribbling away on "these my worthlesse papers torne with Rats."[3]

The "worthlesse papers" gradually became Raleigh's *History of the World,* published anonymously in 1614 as the warrior-poet was entering the second decade of his incarceration. An admirer of Plutarch (whose works had been translated into English by Thomas North in 1579), Raleigh wisely decided, like Shakespeare, not to make his history

---

8. Biography's first martyr. Title page of Sir Walter Raleigh's *Historie of the World* (1614), with an engraved portrait of the warrior-poet and courtier by Simon de Passe. Composed while Raleigh was incarcerated in the Tower of London, the *Historie* was banned by King James I as being "too sawcie in censuring princes." In 1618 Raleigh was executed. Dutch edition, early seventeenth century. *Copyright © Private collection / Bridgeman Art Library.*

too up-to-date; indeed, he halted it at 168 B.C. "I know," declared Raleigh in his preface, "that it will be said by many, That I might haue beene more pleasing to the Reader, if I had written the Story of mine owne times; hauing been permitted to draw water as near the Welle-head as another. To this I answere that who-so-euer in writing a modern Historie, shall follow truth too neare the heeles, it may happily strike out his teeth. There is no Mistresse or Guide, that hath led her followers and seruants into greater miseries."[4]

Biography's First Martyr

The caution did Raleigh no good, nor did his repeated, fawning flatteries of his monarch, James I—"Of whom I may say it truly," he wrote untruthfully, "That if all the malice of the world were infused into one eie: yet could it not discerne in His life, euen to this day, any one of those foule spots, by which the Consciences of all the forenamed Princes (in effect) haue been defiled; nor any droppe of that innocent bloud on the sword of his iustice, with which the most that fore-went him, hauue stayned both their hands and fame."[5]

Far from being mollified, James I had become alarmed when *The History of the World* became a best-seller. He quickly had the book suppressed "for divers exceptions" which he took umbrage at, "but specially for being too sawcie in censuring princes."[6]

After thirteen years Raleigh was finally released from the Tower, but only for a brief respite. Though he'd halted his history before Christ, at the end of Part I, he had not only penned a damning preface excoriating modern kings, but in the body of the text had drawn continual, if implicit parallels between ancient figures and contemporary ones—such as his portrait of the irresolute King Rehoboam, who was "transported by his familiars and fauorites," as well as Queen Semiramis, whose incompetent successor, Ninias, was "esteemed no man of war at all, but altogether feminine, and subjected to ease and delicacy."

The foppish James I, as a practicing homosexual, was not amused. Tried this time for *anti*-Spanish activities—namely, a failed campaign against the Spanish in Guiana, and attempted flight from England thereafter—Raleigh was convicted by a kangaroo court as a sop to the Spanish ambassador. He was taken to the scaffold the following day, October 29, 1618. There he was ordered to place his head upon the block. He is reported to have "desired the headsman to shew him the Axe, which not being suddenly granted to him, he said I prithee, let me see it, dost thou thinke that I am afraid of it, so it being given to him, he felt upon the edge of it, and smiling, spake unto M.

---∞∞∞---

Sir Walter Raleigh's letter to his wife, before his expected execution at the Tower of London in 1603 (reprieved, he was beheaded in 1618):

To what friend to direct you I know not, for all mine have left me in the true time of tryall; most sorry I am (as God knoweth) that being thus surprised with death I can leave you no better estate; I meant you all my Office of wines or that I should purchase by selling it, halfe my stuffe and my jewels (but some for the boy), but God hath prevented all my determinations; The great God that worketh in all.

But if you can live free from want, care for no more, for the rest is but vanity.

Love God, and begin betime to repose your selfe on him, therein shall you finde true and everlasting riches and endlesse comfort: for the rest when you have travelled and wearied your thoughts over all sorts of worldly cogitations, you shall sit downe by sorrow in the end.

Teach your son also to serve and fear God whilst he is young, that the feare of God may grow up with him, then will God be a husband unto you, and a father unto him, a husband and a father that can never be taken from you.

Bayly oweth me 1000 l. Arion 600 l. In Iersie also I have much owing me; the arrerages of the wines will pay your debts.

And howsoever (I beseech you for my soules sake) pay all poore men when I am gone: no doubt you shall bee sought unto, for the world thinks I was very rich.

But take heed of the pretence of men and of their affections, for they last but in honest and worthy men: and no greater misery can befall you in this life, then to become a prey, and after to bee despised: I speake it (God knoweth) not to disswade you from marriage, for that will be best for you, both in respect of God and the world.

As for me I am no more yours, nor you mine, death hath cut us asunder, and God hath divided me from the world, and you from me: Remember your poore childe for his fathers sake that comforted you, and loved you in his happiest times.

I sued for my life (But God knowes) it was for you and yours that I desired it: for know it (deare wife) that your sonne is the childe of a true man, and who in his owne heart despiseth death, and his misshapen and ugly forms.

I cannot write much: God knoweth how hardly I stole this time when all were asleep, and it is now time to separate my thoughts from the world. Beg my dead body which living was denied you, and either lay it in Sherborne or in Exeter Church by my father and mother. I can say no more, time and death call me away. The everlasting God, infinite, powerfull, and inscrutable God, That Almighty God which is goodnesse it selfe, mercy it selfe, the true light and life, keep you and yours, and have mercy upon me.

Sheriffe saying, this is a sharpe medecine, but it is a physician that will cure all diseases."[7]

Biography had its first martyr.

Between the Bed and the Grave

Drawing close parallels between past kings and the reigning monarch had cost Sir Walter Raleigh his head. It was a warning to other, would-be biographers—and taken as such.

Teach me to forgive my persecuters and false accusers, and send me to meet him in his glorious Kingdome.

My true wife farewell, God blesse my poore boy, pray for me, my true God hold you both in His Armes.

> First published as *"To day a man, To morrow none,* OR, SIR Walter Ravvleighs Farewell to his LADY, The night before hee was beheaded: Together with his advice concerning HER, and her SONNE" (London: Printed for R. H., 1644). Renascence editions: darkwing.uoregon.edu.

Faced with the carrot of commemoration and the stick of punishment—even execution—biographers for the most part avoided controversial, critical portraiture and contented themselves with plainsong histories of individuals rather than critical or speculative attempts to penetrate their souls.

In the preface to his *History of the World,* Raleigh had derided fellow biographers who merely "flatter the world, between the bed and the grave."[8] Though his secular martyrdom did nothing to improve matters, his insights still have relevance today. Better than any previous or contemporary author, he'd seen that writing lives was a two-way process: an opportunity for curious minds to visit the past, using current insight into the nature of human conduct to test their understanding of historical figures; but a chance, also, to do the opposite. As Raleigh put it: "In speaking of the past, I point at the present, and taxe the vices of those that are yet lyuing, in their persons that are long since dead."[9]

In other words, even *historical* biography had a *current* subversive agenda—in distinct opposition to the encomium. The personal, in Raleigh's view, *was* the political—involving moral and political censure. It was this agenda, with the eclipse of the Elizabethans, that exercised a nation now speeding toward civil war and its aftermath—Dictatorship, Restoration, Glorious Revolution, and Empire.

Separating the Sheep from the Wolves

Raleigh had been mercilessly executed, but, as he had pointed out in his great history, the study of past figures allows us to gain perspective. Death comes even to tyrants, for "there is no man so assured of his honour, of his riches, health, or life but that he may be depriued of either or all, the very next houre or day to come."[10]

The son of the man who had ordered Raleigh's execution was Charles I. Like Raleigh, King Charles was, in due course, beheaded, while James's grandson, James II, was chased at sword- and gunpoint from his kingdom for the rest of his unhappy life. As in ancient Greece, the merits of republicanism versus kingship, constitutional democracy versus dictatorship (under Oliver Cromwell) were being rehearsed upon a contemporary stage—and though biographers remained under threat of execution if they criticized all-powerful rulers, it became impossible for biographical portraitists to hold to a flattering line in Britain, when the line was constantly moving.

After almost a thousand years of deference to church and state authority, biographers were, once again, called upon not only to commemorate but to take up the Greco-Roman torch and make judgments—political, social, religious, and personal—on their fellow men, as well as their forefathers: separating, as Raleigh saw it, the sheep from the wolves.

The Biographer's Job

Within the great whitestone walls of the Tower, Raleigh had perceived another intrinsic merit of courageous biographical depiction: namely, the very diversity of opinion and interpretation possible in judging an individual. It was not "Truth, but Opinion, that can trauvaile the worlde without a passport," he had remarked in 1614. "For were it otherwise; and were there not as many internall formes of the minde, as there are externall figures of men; there were then some possibility, to perswade by the mouth of one Advocate, even Equity alone."

Just as one might cast around and marvel at the differences between one's fellow men, so, Raleigh argued, the historical chronicler must be willing to allow not only for the physical differences of past individuals, but also for the differences in their *minds*.

> [Among] those that were, of whom we reade and heare, and among those that are, whom we see and conuerse with; every one hath received a seuerall picture of face, and euerie one a diuerse picture of minde; euery one a forme apart, euery one a fancy and cogitation differing: there being nothing wherein Nature so much triumpheth, as in its dissimilitude. From whence it commeth, that there is found so great diuersity of opinions; so strong a contrariety of inclinations; so many naturall and vnnatural; wise, foolish; manly, and childish affections, and passions in Mortall Men. For it is not the visible fashion and shape of plants, and of reasonable Creatures, that

makes the difference, of working in the one, and of condition in the other; but the forme internall.[11]

Only God had mastery of the art of "reading mens thoughts to himselfe," Raleigh allowed; "yet, as the fruit tels the name of the Tree; so the outward workes of men (so farre as their cogitations are acted) give vs wherof to guess the rest. Nay, it were not hard to expresse the one by the other, very neare the life," he remarked—were it not for the fact that "craft in many, feare in the most, and the worlds loue in all" tended "to qualifie and maske over their inward deformities for a time."[12]

It was thus, Raleigh argued, the biographer's *job* to use his detective skills to see through these human masks: examining, especially, the documented sayings of men in order to see into their souls. For, he noted—deliciously quoting his forebear Plutarch—"Neither can any man so change himselfe, but that his heart may be sometimes seene at his tongues end."[13]

Biography Gets a Name

Whether in terms of courageous poet-dramatists like Shakespeare, or poet-chroniclers like Raleigh, sixteenth- and seventeenth-century biographical portraiture in Britain was thus wonderfully enriched, as biographical artists

felt a new spur—so long as they could avoid the executioner's axe—to guess at the minds as well as the actions
and appearances of real individuals in history. In a word, to
interpret.

As a result, life depictions grew in quantity, quality,
and variety, from journalistic pamphlets to multivolume
tomes—rarely, however, daring to be subversive. As a result, the new words coined for practitioners of biography
connoted commemoration, not interpretive work. The
word "biographist," for example, was first used in English
by Thomas Fuller in his *History of the Worthies of England*
(1662), while Bishop Gauden (possible author of the *Eikon
Basilike,* King Charles I's last meditations) coined the alternative, more English-sounding term "biographer" in the
same year. Meanwhile, the term "a biography," the word
used to describe a specific work of written life depiction,
had already become fashionable—used in an anonymous
life of Thomas Fuller in 1661, for example, as well as in
an anonymous "biography" of Oliver Cromwell in 1663—
none of these first usages, sadly, evincing anything but
worthiness.[14]

The unfortunate confusion between specific and generic—between "*a* biography," as *a* chronicle of a specific
life, usually commemorative, on the one hand, and "biography" in general as the whole *field* of life depiction or

study of the real individual, denoting the generic under-taking in Western society—was now approaching. Indeed, it was the dramatist John Dryden who, in 1683, first re-ferred to "biography" as a *collective* noun. Dryden was de-scribing Plutarch's *Lives,* which he had translated, and in so doing referred to the field of "biography" as the "history of particular men's lives."

Dryden had meant only to distinguish between printed life histories and histories of nations. "History of particu-lar men's lives" was, however, a phrase that, once seized upon by lexicographers, would soon attain an almost in-delible influence on the way the public saw the previous three thousand years of life depiction—a neat definition, in their patriarchal, ink-stained hands: one that excluded women, and that implied only *written* history of lives.

How? For three millennia almost no one had sought to limit the business of life depiction to a single word, or a single genre. Roger North, in his unpublished preface to *The Life of the Lord Keeper North,* had set down perhaps the best late seventeenth-century reflections on the art prac-ticed by "lifewriters" such as himself, as well as "idiogra-phy," or "notes of me."[15] In the growing Enlightenment mania for scientific taxonomies, however, "lifewriting" was not considered sharp enough. Thus, the translation of the Latin word *biographus* as "*a* biography," and the limitation of "biographies" to *written*, printed histories of *men*, was perhaps inevitable. Poor Dryden was given the dubious honor of being the first to use the generic term—despite the fact that his phrase had been taken out of the context of biographical compilers, in a discussion of Plutarch.

This was, in terms of the study of biography as life depiction rather than lifewriting, an epistemological misfortune whose ramifications would continue to the present day—despite the invention of film, radio, television, and the Internet. Although the Enlightenment dictionary definition of "biography" did at least reestablish the legitimacy of critical secular life depiction, as opposed to hagiography, it also served to limit the public's understanding of the notion of life depiction in general. "Biography" did not become the *study* of real individuals, across the whole spectrum of arts, but was defined and confined to "written histories" only—thus steering the notion of life representation further along the path established by Gutenberg and Caxton, but away from the Globe Theater.

As a generic noun, "biography" would, henceforth, be locked up and the key cast away—the term guarded by compilers (male) of English dictionaries in a logobox whose woodenness and square corners did scant justice to three thousand years of the depiction of real individuals, in every conceivable medium.

Logotypecasting

The result of such logotypecasting, sadly, was the relegation of the study of human lives to mere histories. It was as if "history," as the study of the past, had been reduced to extant works of historianship. In a society freed from the chains of both the church and the state (which until the 1660s had had the right to approve writings before permission to print was granted), the newly coined word "biography" thus became synonymous only with worthy book depictions of real people: printed texts, rather than studies of individuals expressed in different media.

However unfortunate the dictionary limitation of the term "biography," the *business* of secular life depiction was, nevertheless, taking off across the whole spectrum of the arts, from paint and marble to engravings and theater. Compilations of print essays certainly prospered—Fuller's *Worthies of England* leading to a host of works that revived the Plutarchian tradition, exemplified in scholarly volumes such as Gerard Langbaine's *Account of the English Dramatick Poets* (1691), family portraits such as Roger North's *Lives of the Norths,* and literary masterpieces such as Isaak Walton's pious but beautifully written *Lives* (recounting the life stories of Donne, Wotton, Hooker, and Herbert), first collected in 1670 and reprinted many times thereafter. John

Aubrey's *four hundred* anecdotally inspired *Brief Lives,* collected between 1669 and 1696, contributed the fresh spice
of intimate, personal detail to what was rapidly becoming
a revived prose genre of compilation—though it should
be remembered that Aubrey, in a small autobiographical
memoir of his own life, noted that the γράφ in "biography" should best be translated as "graphic," or in his case,
"geometrie," wherein rested his chief interest. "If ever I
had been good for anything, 'twould have been a painter, I
could fancy a thing so strongly and had so cleare an idea of
it," Aubrey wrote. As a child, he recalled, he "gave himselfe
to drawing and painting." He was and remained, he concluded, not so much a biographer as a "portraiter."[16]

Misusing the Term

For centuries religious iconography had literally illumi-
nated life depiction, alongside hagiographic texts. Now, in
an England more and more secular since the Reformation,
portraiture of *secular* individuals—whether in paint, plas-
ter, or bronze, whether on the stage or in print—rivaled
and finally eclipsed religious life depictions. Sadly, this development was not encompassed in the new word "biography." How ironic, therefore, that the origin of the generic word "biography" should have been pinned upon
John Dryden—one of the finest eighteenth-century dra-

matists and satirists. As critic, poet, playwright, theologian, translator, political philosopher, and essayist, Dryden would have turned in his grave had he known how later academics, lexicographers, and others would misuse his term: for to him life depiction was the study of the stories of men in the context of their lives and times, in *all* media—poetry, plays, paint, print.

As it turned out, it would take almost three hundred years to extend the word "biography" to encompass the many possible forms of life depiction—and to cover women. In the meantime, however, a giant now strode upon the English biographical stage, someone whose opinions would provide a vision of the modern *purpose* of biography that has lasted to this day: Samuel Johnson.

Life versus Panegyric

Such was the unfettered, proliferating fascination with real lives in the early eighteenth century that the reading public had become progressively unwilling to wait for scholarly writers to produce book lives—"biographies"—of contemporary figures. *Journalists* therefore willingly stepped forward into the breach. By 1715, two years after publication of his own blank-verse drama based on the life of Marcus Porcius Cato of Utica (95–46 B.C.), the poet-playwright-essayist-critic-biographer Joseph Addison complained in *The*

Freeholder about his fellow "Grub Street biographers," who were increasingly wont to "watch for the death of a Great Man." Biographers, in other words, were functioning as extended newspaper obituarists.

The reason journalists hesitated to print biographical accounts of *living* subjects was simple: the law of defamation and libel imposed severe penalties on writers who deliberately or inadvertently marred the reputation of living individuals. The death of an individual, however, released writers from any legal requirement to preserve his or her reputation—so journalists, taking advantage of a new and burgeoning market, sharpened their quills accordingly. It was William Oldyss who coined the adjective "biographical"—using it in his new print biography, *Life of Walter Ralegh* (1738), to sneer at his fellow "biographical fry," who, he lamented, had "nibbled at" his idealized, executed hero. (Raleigh, of course, would have welcomed such licensed frying, on so many stages and across so many pages, for it signified not only the "great discord and dissimilitude of reasonable creatures," as he put it, but also the colorfulness of opinions.[17] He quoted a dictum of Seneca's: "Mala opinio, bene parta, delectat": "A bad reputation is delightful, if virtuously acquired.")

Given this profusion of new and varying opinions and

depictions of reputations, especially by journalists, it was left to the great literary doctor of mid-eighteenth-century letters to bring his renowned intellect to bear on the business of critical biography.

Samuel Johnson was fascinated by the lives of poets—if only because his own attempts to write verse had proved miserable failures. Writing biographical essays, by contrast, enabled him to use his intellect, his wit, and a range of compassion and critical judgment that raised him above the "biographical fry." To exercise this critical judgment, however, it was important for him to release biography from the restraints of encomium. "If a man is to write *A Panegyrick*," Johnson memorably advised his own biographer, James Boswell, "he may keep vices out of sight, but if he professes to write *A Life* he must represent it really as it was."[18]

Later historians, following Leopold von Ranke ("wie es eigentlich gewesen [ist]"—"as it actually was"), would have cause to remember this latter phrase, but for serious writers in the eighteenth century the exhortation to cast off the shackles of encomium and ethical hero-worship came at an opportune moment, in a burgeoning middle-class society hungry for knowledge and more reading materials. Quoting the Latin poet Horace, Johnson called for life de-

9. Dr. Samuel Johnson (1709–1784) became the philosopher-father of modern literary biography, through his writings in his twice-weekly twopenny magazine, *The Rambler*, and in his *Lives of the Poets*. Here, Henry Wallis' 1854 oil portrait depicts Johnson at work on *The Rambler* in Edward Cave's printing office. Being too poor to appear at Cave's table, he had his food brought to him behind a screen. *Copyright © Private collection / Bridgeman Art Library.*

pictions that included elements both "beautiful and base," embracing "vice and virtue," rather than relying on the "sober sages of the schools."

It was not that, as a staid conservative, Johnson ignored the pedagogic, educational importance of learning about past persons; rather, it was his secular objection to the staple reading of the Middle Ages, hagiography or the Lives of the Saints, that impelled him to protest. Reading about people who did no wrong, or made no mistakes, was fatuous, he felt. "If nothing but the bright side of characters should be shewn," he pointed out, "we should sit down in despondency, and think it utterly impossible to imitate them in *any thing.*"[19] By an "act of imagination," modern biographers should instead present narratives that would permit readers to witness, at one remove, the "joys and calamities of others, however fictitious"—for the purpose of biography was, he recognized, to allow the audience to empathize with, or project onto, the life portrayed.

"Our passions are therefore strongly moved," Johnson remarked, once the audience recognizes the "pains or pleasures of others." Indeed, so important did this biographical *identification* appear to Johnson that he downgraded the study of history in favor of biography. "Histories of the downfall of kingdoms, and revolutions of empires" could never, he claimed, provide the same human insight and therapeutic benefit as biography. Historians were, as a breed, simply not up to such an education of the senses, since their narratives necessarily involved "a thousand fortunes in the business of a day."[20] As Johnson memorably added, "the most artful writer" was thus called to respond to a crucial challenge: how to move "the man whose faculties have been engrossed by business, and whose heart never fluttered but at the rise or fall of stocks"—a man who "wonders how the attention can be seized, or the affections agitated by a tale of love."[21]

Dr. Johnson's Vision

Appealing to his fellow biographers to end idle idealization, Johnson thus demanded a frank biographical account of "the mistakes and miscarriages, escapes and expedients" of the subject's life story, so well recounted that the reader would be able to draw for himself the human lessons "common to human kind"—however distinctive the "adventures and separable decorations and disguises" of the biographee.[22]

Biography was, for Johnson, a deeply modern cause—in fact, he was said to love most "the biographical part of literature," as his *Lives of the Poets* demonstrated. Despite being the quintessential intellectual, he was, like Suetonius, curious always about the distinctive mannerisms, eccentricities, and particularities of a subject that allowed an outsider to see the human being within the vestments and achievements of a personality. He thus found himself disappointed by many of the prose portraits drawn by his contemporaries. Biographers, he famously wrote, "so little regard the manners or behaviour of their heroes, that more knowledge may be gained of a man's real character, by a short conversation with one of his servants, than from a formal and studied narrative, begun with his pedigree, and ended with his funeral."[23]

Johnson's new valuation of biography would have a powerful impact on his contemporaries—not only spawning Boswell's great *Life of Samuel Johnson, LL.D.*, but Oliver Goldsmith's immortal remark when asked what was the best lesson for youth. "The life of a good man," Goldsmith replied. Pressed to give the next best lesson, he retorted: "The life of a bad one."[24]

Reinstating Color

The *Life of Samuel Johnson, LL.D.*, published in 1791 by his companion, James Boswell—diarist, interviewer, and inveterate rake—provided a classic example of the new warts-and-all biography: messy, vivid, and colorful as life itself.

Edmund Curll, a London publisher, had made a fortune printing "intimate, anecdotal, scurrilous" lives of "famous and notorious persons who had the ill-fortune to die during his life-time," as one literary essayist later remarked.[25] Yet so lively and interesting was Boswell's effort that, as Richard Altick later commented, Boswell "elevated large-

———— ❧ ————

Boswell's final summary, at the end of his famous 1791 biography of his mentor and friend Dr. Johnson:

The character of SAMUEL JOHNSON has, I trust, been so developed in the course of this work, that they who have honoured it with a perusal, may be considered as well acquainted with him. As, however, it may be expected that I should collect into one view the capital and distinguishing features of this extraordinary man, I shall endeavour to acquit myself of that part of my biographical undertaking, however difficult it may be to do that which many of my readers will do better for themselves.

His figure was large and well-formed, and his countenance of the cast of an ancient statue, yet his appearance was rendered strange and somewhat uncouth, by convulsive cramps, by the scars of that distemper which it was once imagined the royal touch could cure, and by a slovenly mode of dress. He had the use of only one eye; yet so much does mind govern and even supply the deficiency of organs, that his visual perceptions, as far as they extended, were uncommonly quick and accurate. So morbid was his temperament, that he never knew the natural joy of a free and vigorous use of his limbs: when he walked, it was like the struggling gait of one in fetters; when he rode, he had no command or direction of his horse, but was carried as if in a balloon. That with his constitution and habits of life he should have lived seventy-five years, is a proof that an inherent vivanda vis is a powerful preservative of the human frame.

Man is in general made up of contradictory qualities, and these will ever show themselves in strange succession.

James Boswell, *The Life of Samuel Johnson, LL.D.* (Ware, U.K.: Wordsworth Editions, 1999), pp. 987–988.

scale biography to a place of dignity in the hierarchy of lit-erary forms"—rescuing it from the "squalid associations that still clung to it from the days of Curll and the Grub Streeters, and made the composition of biographies a liter-ary activity in which the most respectable writers could unapologetically engage."[26]

"Unapologetically" was perhaps an exaggeration. While readers were won over by the vivacity of Boswell's multi-layered portrait, they were not entirely won over by the libertine author—or his intimate revelations about John-son. What was truly a return to Roman biographies, how-ever, was Boswell's incorporation of journalistic, gossipy detail and color within his account of Dr. Johnson's profes-sional life story, designed as it was to balance the some-what heavy, even tedious and predictably noble character of his hero. By spending so much time with Johnson, and noting not only the great man's sayings but the detailed *settings* in which they were delivered, Boswell indelibly por-trayed the Doctor for posterity—and in a way that Johnson himself could never have done, autobiographically, despite his own *Lives of the Poets*.

Letters, Diaries, Journals—and Autobiography

Boswell's was not the only master *oeuvre* of Enlightenment life depiction. A fashion for letters, diaries, and journals swept Europe—indeed, no middle-class home was without its writing-table. Self-reflection was not considered narcissistic; rather, it was painted and penned for self-improvement. Autobiographies likewise proliferated under the more secular, liberal conditions of the time—culminating in a Swiss philosopher's unsaintly, posthumous memoirs, modeled on Saint Augustine's great confession to God, but without the benefit of deity: these were the *Confessions* of Jean-Jacques Rousseau, published in 1781, three years after his death.

Augustine had remained a model autobiographer for Catholics for many centuries. As the church's religious constraints on European literacy lessened with the Reformation, however, the confessional was literally and figuratively cast out by Protestants, who resented the mediation of priests between man and God. Yet such a powerful channel for expressing a human emotion as deeply intimate as guilt could not become completely redundant—and it didn't, as secular writers warmed to the confessional form. In secular hands, autobiographical dialogue became, once again, a direct communication, this time between author and reader, held back only by decorum: what an individual was permitted, given the mores of the time, to reveal about himself or herself. Montaigne had perfected such a dialogue in the sixteenth century—indeed, he invented what would be known as the personal essay, in which the author meditates on his personal experience as experience, rather than as a tribute to divinity—done both "for a nook in the library," as Montaigne put it, and "to amuse a neighbor, a relative, a friend, who may take pleasure in associating and conversing with me again in this image."[27]

A dialogue of this type was thus a secular appeal to a secular market—and it was in this context that Rousseau's confessions put autobiography on the literary rather than the memoirist or religious map.

Rousseau Confesses

"I am commencing an undertaking," Rousseau began his *chef-d'oeuvre*, "hitherto without precedent, and which will never find an imitator. I desire to set before my fellows the likeness of a man in all the truth of nature, and that man is myself.

"Myself alone! I know the feelings of my heart, and I know men. I am not made like any of those I have seen; I venture to believe that I am not made like any of those who are in existence. If I am not better, at least I am different. Whether nature has acted rightly or wrongly in destroying the mould in which she cast me, can only be decided after I am dead."

In his *Confessions,* Rousseau professed himself to be almost completely uninterested in God. Lacking the modesty of Montaigne, his admissions were aimed *directly* to those other individuals in the metaphorical reading room: individuals who might be converted to liking—or at least appreciating—him for his relentless honesty and self-lacerating self-aggrandizement. "See if *you* could be as truthful!" was Rousseau's candid, always implicit, sometimes explicit challenge to the reader as he indulged in embarrassing self-flagellation—a challenge that has served to lash the beast not only of confessional autobiographies but of biographies, too, ever since.

For all that Rousseau reestablished the questing confessional narrative, or questioning *power* of autobiography, in form and content (especially his uninhibited account of his sexual development), his *Confessions* could not and did not tell more than one side of the Rousseau story, or even the verifiable truth—a limitation that has always been the Achilles heel of autobiographical work.

In the *Confessions,* Rousseau admitted, for example, that by the mid-1760s he had already stopped having sex with his mistress Thérèse for several years, after she had borne a number of his children—who were promptly given to a Foundling Hospital. For sexual release he had then relied on masturbation—ostensibly for the sake of his health: "I

had observed that intercourse with women distinctly aggravated my ill-health; the corresponding vice, of which I
have never been able to cure myself completely, appeared
to me to produce less injurious results."[28] As a result of
such onanism, he had "observed a coldness on the part of
Thérèse," but he did not, in his autobiography, ask himself
whether she had found the same or other medicine for her
own ill-health. Only when James Boswell's *Journals,* mislaid
after his death, were published almost two hundred years
later, in the 1950s, did it become clear that Thérèse, preparing to follow Rousseau from Paris to his exile in England,
had indulged herself in her own way, given Rousseau's
willful "continence." Young Boswell, too, happened to be
on his way to Britain, returning home after the sudden
death of his mother, Lady Auchinleck. As Adam Sisman
has described in his vivid biography, *Boswell's Presumptu-
ous Task,* based on Boswell's *Journals,* it was arranged that
Boz, who had encountered Rousseau in Switzerland and
Corsica, should escort Thérèse personally. "To pass the
time during the trip, the forty-five-year-old Thérèse offered
the young man a "lesson in the art of love." By the time
they reached Dover, Boswell boasted, they had "done it"
thirteen times.

Fact—or fiction? Who can know, either from Rousseau's
public confessions or Boswell's private ones? Neither man,

however, had penned his record as fiction, or intended it to be read as such. Using the same documentary raw materials of conventional biographies (memory, diaries, journals, memoranda, correspondence, and reported speech, whether remembered or taken down in interviews), their autobiographical writings were self-conscious, nonfictional life depictions of themselves; indeed, both men were outraged whenever their truthfulness was impugned. They accepted that it might be difficult to be entirely truthful about oneself—but they were *trying*.

CHAPTER 4

Victorian Pseudobiography

With the British yoke undone in the American Revolution of 1776 and the overthrow of the *ancien régime* in the French Revolution of 1789, it was perhaps small wonder that the newly labeled art of autobiography was at the literary forefront of life depiction. Not only were revolutionaries of interest to the world, but they could even paint their own life stories without waiting for posthumous biographers to do so.

In a New World of autodidacts and articulate personal witnesses to world-altering events, autobiographers led the biographical way, quickly establishing autobiography as a challenging, populist field of belles lettres, incorporating four areas of special expertise: memoir, apologia, essay, and confessional. In a Western Hemisphere turned upside down by political and social insurrection, with a new emphasis on the rights of the individual and a growing interest in the *self* of that individual, autobiography offered the reader a double benefit: on the one hand, personal testimony relating to great events and individuals, and, on the other, an intimate, licensed spotlight into the individual human psyche.

The Romantics, especially, took up this torch—seizing and extending the autobiographical form in poetry, prose, painting, sculpture. As Sir Walter Scott wrote in 1808, "The present age has discovered a desire, or rather a rage, for literary anecdote and private history."[1] It was the wave of the future—and in that respect as in others, the fledgling United States constituted the future.

"Autobiography may be the preeminent kind of American expression," Henry James later claimed ironically— ironically since, as a self-appointed exile living in England and in denial of his "inverted" self, James was the natural enemy of overt and revealing self-depiction. An acute observer of the human drama, James was being prophetic, but responding, too, to "prophetic autobiography"—a genre that had characterized self-depiction in America since its Puritan origins. Without the reassuring historical identity of Europeans, the white émigrés who colonized America and created the USA proved initially as self-hagiographic as the saints of Europe: they were men and women who believed implicitly that the individual, their free churches, and the colonies shared a special role in man's redemption. It was therefore not surprising that the Mormon revelation of 1830 should have taken place in America.[2] In the fluid, relatively classless society of the New World—at least, in comparison with the society of the Old World—such revelations found fertile soil, as did other autobiographical claims and testimony, both religious and secular—forcing Americans to test their new beliefs and identities in a unique, pioneering way that still characterizes American autobiography today—at once brash and humble, challenging and mythological, community-obsessed and individualistic. Their own personal experience, however humble, and those of others near them in space and time, rather than history and high birth, was crucial to their self-worth, leading them to speak and write frankly and with relatively little inhibition—and forming, in book after book through the nineteenth century and into the twentieth, a paperchain of unabashed self-depiction.

A bibliographic-genealogical line would thus connect the auto-testimonies of Benjamin Franklin with the travails and quests of Henry David Thoreau and Frederick Douglass, and beyond them Gertrude Stein, Malcolm X, and Norman Mailer: a sense that, even if personally unable to change the world through action, such authors might change it by the force of autobiographical narrative.

Meanwhile, in Europe, confessional autobiographies built upon another literary habit that went hand-in-hand with increasing literacy: the keeping of diaries. Here, autobiography could be practiced en masse, whether by schoolchildren or by Romantic poets making notes for later versification—thereby providing the richest materials for later historians and sociologists. Romantics, moreover, were well aware of such afterlife for their jottings, however temporarily private. In his *Detached Notes,* Byron bared all, or almost all, from homosocial loves to bawdy conquests. But "I must not go on with these reflections," he mused on August 23, 1819, "or I shall be letting out some secret or other to paralyse posterity."[3]

Autobiography had thus become, by the age of the steam engine, the new propellant of biography in modern individualistic Western society. As André Maurois later remarked in his Clark lectures at Cambridge, after quoting from Byron's Ravenna journal at the point where the pistol-toting poet set out on his "somewhat perilous, but not disagreeable" search for sex: "I would willingly give the lives of Byron by Moore and Elze and Edgcumbe and all the rest, even Trelawny, for a few such pages of the diary."[4]

The Sullen Cloud

To this day, historians of biography are still not quite sure why written, painted, sculpted, and theatrically dramatized real-life depiction, so clearly on the cusp of a fourth golden age with the dawn of Romanticism, so swiftly "faded into humdrum performance, pseudobiography," as Paul Murray Kendall would write in his *Art of Biography.*[5]

Why? How? Had not Jean-Jacques Rousseau, in 1776, written his own counter-biography, *Rousseau: Judge of Jean-Jacques?* Had not Napoleon, a former artillery cadet, made himself master of Europe and an emperor? Had not the American colonies risen up and invented a new basis for democratic society? Had not Beethoven composed his great Ninth Symphony? Had not Goethe and Schiller, through *Sturm und Drang,* opened up the floodgates of Romanticism, with its reverence for nature, its belief in individual-

---

10. "Mad, bad—and dangerous to know": this is the way Lady Caroline Lamb summed up Lord Byron, who was, and remained, the most notorious poet of the Romantic era, his diaries and letters only adding to his fame. Max Beerbohm's 1904 engraved cartoon depicts him shaking off the dust of England (as well as debts and rumors of incest) on his departure from the country forever in 1816. *Copyright © Central St. Martin's College of Art and Design / Bridgeman Art Library.*

—∞∞∞—

An excerpt from Byron's "Ravenna journal," or diary, for January 4, 1821 (written at the time Byron was hoping for an Italian insurrection against the Austrians):

This morning I gat me up late, as usual—weather bad—bad as England—worse. The snow of last week melting to the sirocco of to-day, so that there were two d—d things at once. Could not even get to ride on horseback in the forest. . . .

I was out of spirits—read the papers—thought what fame was, on reading, in a case of murder, that "Mr. Wych, grocer, at Tunbridge, sold some bacon, flour, cheese, and, it is believed, some plums, to some gypsy woman accused. He had on his counter (I quote faithfully) a book, the Life of Pamela, which he was tearing for waste paper, &c., &c. In the cheese was found, &c., and a leaf of Pamela wrapt round the bacon." What would Richardson, the vainest and luckiest of living authors (i.e., while alive)—he who, with Aaron Hill, used to prophesy and chuckle over the presumed fall of Fielding (the prose Homer of human nature) and of Pope (the most beautiful of poets)—what would he have said, could he have traced his pages from their place on the French prince's toilets (see Boswell's Johnson) to the grocer's counter and the gipsy-murderess's bacon!!! What would he have said? What can anybody say, save what Solomon said long before us? After all, it is but passing from one counter to another, from the bookseller's to the other trades-man's grocer or pastry-cook. For my part, I have met with most poetry upon trunks; so that I am apt to consider the trunk-maker as the sexton of authorship.

Byron's Letters and Journals, vol. 8: *Born for Opposition, 1821*, ed. Leslie A. Marchand (Cambridge, Mass.: Harvard University Press, 1978), pp. 11–12.

ism and unconventional mysticism, opposition to political tyranny, exaltation of passion, fascination with the morbid, love of emotion for its own sake? Had not the scandalous Lord Byron stirred the excitement of a new generation, and De Quincey penned his remarkable 1822 *Confessions of an English Opium Eater?* The latter beginning with his memorable apology:

> I here present you, courteous reader, with the record of a remarkable period of my life; according to my application of it, I trust that it will prove, not merely an interesting record, but, in a considerable degree, useful and instructive. In *that* hope it is that I have drawn it up; and *that* must be my apology for breaking through that delicate and honourable reserve, which, for the most part, restrains us from the public exposure of our own errors and infirmities. Nothing, indeed, is more revolting to English feelings, than the spectacle of a human being obtruding on our notice his moral ulcers, or scars, and tearing away that "decent drapery" which time, or indulgence to human frailty, may have drawn over them.[6]

Were not De Quincey's tortured self-revelations but part of *twenty-four volumes* of autobiographical essays—a testament, if any was needed, to biography's galloping inflation in the early nineteenth century, drawing back the "decent drapery," and spurred on by biographers and autobiographers of every background and predilection?

Yet after a period in which every lover kept not only a diary but his mistress's letters and her locks, and every reader read Shelley, Keats, Coleridge as well as the promiscuous author of *Don Juan,* the vibrant, challengingly *real* life seemed to go out of life depiction. As Harold Nicolson later remarked: "Then came earnestness, and with earnestness hagiography descended on us with its sullen cloud, and the Victorian biographer scribbled laboriously by the light of shaded lamps."[7] As did the Victorian painter, sculptor, and dramatist.

Why?

Renewed Encomia

Even today we can only speculate on what prompted the years of cultural as well as political reaction. Moreover—as historians of printed lives have shown—there was no diminution in biographical output in Britain following the accession of young Queen Victoria, or in America after Andrew Jackson.[8] On the contrary: in an age of increasing literacy, the public appetite for biography grew exponentially. But so, too, did Victorian evangelism, fear of poverty, and moralizing. Confessional accounts like Harriette Wilson's *Memoirs* of 1825 became unreprintable in Victorian England, which condemned confessional authors like "Walter," writing in the footsteps of Giacomo Casanova's untranslated *History of My Life* a century earlier,[9] to write only for private publication. (Such works targeted a sophisticated, literary middle class able to afford the price of a specially printed and bound edition that was labeled "pornography" by the Victorians—in contrast to permitted "autobiography.")

De Quincey, as an Englishman, had assumed that his confession of drug addiction would have to await publication after his death, in another age—aware that "for any such acts of gratuitous self-humiliation from those who can be supposed in sympathy with the decent and self-respecting part of society, we must look to French literature, or to that part of the German which is tainted with the spurious and defective sensibility of the French." Romanticism, however, had empowered him to publish and thereby risk being damned—whereas, had he waited until after his death in 1859, as we shall see, it is unlikely his heirs would have allowed the "impropriety" of such revelations.

Following the demise of Romanticism, then, the por-

trayal of real (rather than fictional) lives inexorably reverted, in the 1840s, to the portraiture of exclusively stal-
wart, worthy people: renewed encomia, for didactic Victorian purposes.

To this, Victorian expansionism added yet *another* burden to biography, since imperialism, too, contributed to
the demand for patriotic and exemplary, rather than honest, lives. The burden consisted in a renewal of Christian life-laundering, though accompanied this time by burgeoning scientific empiricism and industry. Knowledge was
good, and was to be promoted via education—but mostly
within a new nationalist spirit, strongly buttressed by evan-
gelical Christianity, which viewed empire not as exploita-
tion of others but as an opportunity for missionary, vice-
less zeal.

Dr. Johnson would have been appalled—but values had
changed. Whereas Raleigh had urged his fellow men, in
the words of Seneca, to "satisfie our own consciences, and
not trouble ourselves with fame," the Victorians came to
care very much about imperial fame. In an era of growing
chasm between rich and poor, "reputation" became a sine
qua non for membership in the upper and middle classes,
permitting members to distinguish and isolate themselves
from the ever-frightening, ever-multiplying poor.

John Gibson Lockhart, official biographer of Sir Walter Scott, writing at the start of the Victorian era, warns against "Boswellizing":

I never thought it lawful to keep a journal of what passes in private society, so that no one need expect from the sequel of this narrative any detailed record of Scott's familiar talk. What fragments of it have happened to adhere to a tolerably retentive memory, and may be put in black and white without wounding any feelings which my friend, were he alive, would have wished to spare, I shall introduce as the occasion suggests or serves. But I disclaim on the threshold any thing more than this; and I also wish to enter a protest once for all against the general fidelity of several literary gentlemen who have kindly forwarded to me

The Sexes Draw Apart

Reputation, as the nineteenth century unfolded, thus became all—lest one sink back into the mire. Suppression of unpalatable facts and of anything injurious to reputation—

private lucubrations of theirs, designed to *Boswellize* Scott, and which they may probably publish hereafter. . . . In proportion as a man is witty and humorous, there will always be about him and his a widening maze and wilderness of cues and catchwords, which the uninitiated will, if they are bold enough to try interpretation, construe, ever and anon, egregiously amiss—not seldom into arrant falsity. For this one reason, to say nothing of many others, I consider no man justified in journalizing what he sees or hears in a domestic circle where he is not thoroughly at home; and I think there are still higher and better reasons why he should not do so where he is.

J. G. Lockhart, *Memoirs of the Life of Sir Walter Scott, Bart*, vol. 4 (New York: William Lewer, 1837), ch. 5, pp. 107–108.

especially sexual episodes—went hand in hand with a rhetoric of evasion and obfuscation: the new hagiography, as Harold Nicolson later called it.

Nicolson's friend Virginia Woolf would also deplore the

way, with the accession of Queen Victoria, the basic features of human existence were doctored. "Love, birth and death" became "swaddled in a variety of fine phrases," while "the sexes drew further apart"—among the upper and middle classes, at least. "No open conversation was tolerated," she lamented. "Evasions and concealments were sedulously practised on both sides. Thus the British Empire came into existence; and thus—for there is no stopping damp; it gets into the inkpot as it gets into the woodwork—sentences multiplied, adjectives multiplied, lyrics became epics, and"—thinking of her father's magisterial *Dictionary of National Biography* of 1886—"little trifles that had been essays a column long were now encyclopaedias in ten or twenty volumes."[10]

Eager to explore and expand the frontiers of human factual comprehension, the Victorians endowed the biographical record of their age with a multitude of forms, from statuary to paintings, lithographs to daguerreotypes, miniatures to photographs, printed encomia to fawning memoirs. As the nineteenth century progressed, however, they seemed to chain themselves, in biography at least, to the very crosses from which Johnson and others had attempted to release them.

The Victorian public, policed by upper- and middle-class magistrates and arbiters of decency and morality, demanded—and for the most part received—spotless reputations. Any mention of sex, beyond the designation of gender, now became a stain. Byron's enforced exile for promiscuity (including a possible relationship with his half-sister Augusta Leigh), rather than for political indiscretions, had pointed the way. Increasingly, biographers left at home in Victorian England came to believe that portraying human beings "really as they were" was an insult to propriety—William Godwin's life of his wife, Mary Wollstonecraft, being a sad but typical casualty. (Telling her true life—*Memoirs of the Author of "A Vindication of the Rights of Woman"*—resulted not in her canonization, as Godwin had hoped, but in her effacement from the canon of the respectable dead, for more than a hundred years.)[11]

A seemingly endless assembly line of factual biographical dictionaries and compendia of distinguished, sexless, almost entirely male lives were produced by hack compilers such as Samuel Smiles. Graphic representations of cleansed figures abounded—leading to the establishment of the National Portrait Gallery in London (in 1856) *specifically* to encourage idealization of achievement through the contemplation of noble biographical example.

Printed life chronicles followed the same principle. Vices were uniformly excluded—to the delight of fictional writers. For them, the failure of print biographers—even portrait painters and other biographical artists—to produce truthful rather than idealized portraits was a heaven-sent opportunity, inspiring them to write the greatest "biographical" novels of all time.

Fictitious Lives

To the lasting credit of Victorian novelists as students of the human individual, it was they, not biographers, who, for good and ill, received the pass and ran with Johnson's ball. With reputation the sine qua non of middle-class citizenship, the responsibility for portraying "vice *and* virtue" now came to rest upon the shoulders of Victorian fiction writers—authors who licensed themselves, in realistic works, to depict alarmingly real yet imaginary lives. Such works ranged from Dickens' *David Copperfield* to Flaubert's *Madame Bovary,* from Brontë's *Jane Eyre* to Gaskell's *Mary Barton,* from Hawthorne's *Scarlet Letter* to Melville's *Moby-Dick,* from Dostoyevsky's *Brothers Karamazov* to Tolstoy's *Anna Karenina,* from Zola's *Nana* to Hardy's *Tess of the D'Urbervilles* and Conrad's *Heart of Darkness* and *Lord Jim.*

Once again, fiction had, like its Greek antecedents, benefited from biographers' chariness and commemorative bent in order to counterbalance well-meaning but less-than-truthful homilies. Courageously taking on the role of "historiographical parasites," as J. R. Morgan, historian of Greek fiction, put it—the descendants of Petronius, Lollianus, and Heliodorus shone their lamps into the "empty corners of real history"[12] in works that gave, and still give, readers (and audiences, when dramatized, televised, or filmed) of all classes a far more vivid insight into past and contemporary society through "other mens forepassed miseries," as Raleigh called them,[13] than any Victorian historian or "biographer" dared. Novelists portrayed all sorts of social ills, from abuse of schoolchildren to incest, patricide, madness, prostitution, and adultery.

Betraying the Johnsonian Ideal

Biography-styled fiction, together with conventional, inhibited biography, may thus best be seen as the *combined* way in which society records and interprets the lives of individuals. Certainly it was in this strange upstairs-downstairs Victorian duet that the study of the individual in society prospered in Victorian Britain and America—a division of labor that would persist almost to the present day as writers of fictional biographies became licensed in Western society to explore what was, by a sort of common social consent, off limits to conventional biographers. By contrast, documentary biographers found themselves expected, indeed required by their publishers, theater managers, and commissioning agents, to adopt the fawning manners of courtiers to their subjects—or rather, superiors.

No Boswell or Rousseau stepped forward to sully this Victorian laundering process—nor would he have been published or produced had he done so. The Johnsonian ideal had simply been cast out of nonfictional life depiction, to be rescued by novelists. Save for a thriving underground press, cartoons, and scurrilous vaudeville theater, the serious, nonfictional portraits produced by Victorian biographical artists and print biographers remained respectful, prolific, unimaginative, ponderous—and pure. Like the more pompous Greek and Roman chroniclers, Victorian biographers believed (or pretended to believe) that the exterior life of a man should be accepted at face value as the clue to his inner life, his soul—their faith in success, and their fear of disorder, chaos, poverty, and the fires of hell, making them unwilling to peer behind the death masks which Raleigh and the great Elizabethan life dramatists such as Shakespeare had warned must first be removed.

Dr. Johnson had been Shakespeare's great champion in the mid-eighteenth century, his "Preface to Shakespeare" being considered perhaps his finest work of prose. Shakespearean honesty and insight, however, were now impermissible in the realm of biography—a new divide between brilliant fiction and unreal, hagiographic nonfictional work characterizing virtually the entire Victorian era. The quality of that biographical writing was summed up in Lytton Strachey's famous quip: "Those two fat volumes, with which it is our custom to commemorate the dead—who does not know them, with their ill-digested masses of material, their slipshod style, their tone of tedious panegyric, their lamentable lack of selection, of detachment, of design? They are as familiar as the *cortège* of the undertaker, and wear the same air of slow, funereal barbarism."[14]

Life of Dickens

Strachey was exaggerating, of course. As cultural archaeologists, we owe the Victorians an immense debt of gratitude, for although they may have laundered their lives, they recorded them in great detail, leaving a vast documentary record that allows us to retrace their lives, just as we renovate their wonderfully solid yet exuberantly individualistic homes. However much they may have wanted to conceal their private lives, their public ones were—and remain—extraordinary in their industry. Explorers, scientists, inventors, evangelists, militarists, pioneers, traders, manufacturers, social philosophers, social engineers, imperialists . . . Strachey may have deplored their fat volumes, but he was as awed by their output as anyone.

11. The precision of photography made it possible to extend the documentary scope of biographical depictions in the nineteenth century. Here, President Abraham Lincoln poses before the camera of Alexander Gardner four days before delivering his Gettysburg Address on November 19, 1863. *Copyright © Private collection / Bridgeman Art Library.*

We should just note, in passing, another development that took place in Victorian times—the result, really, of the burgeoning Victorian economy. It was a development that to a great extent molded the face of biography in its various forms: the rise of the new *profession* of "biographer."

Commissioned portrait painters had been known for centuries, but it was in Victorian times that writers came forward to pen *paid* lives. These were men (and sometimes women) willing and able to produce, for money, laundered life stories: commissioned biography, or literary portraiture.

Sadly, given the continuing state of patriarchy in the Western (as in the Asian and African) world, patrons willingly spent fortunes on prettified portraits of their mistresses and wives, but for the most part commissioned biographers to record lives only of *men*—with occasional exceptions for female monarchs such as Queen Victoria.

A typical such professional "biographer" was John Forster: a journalist by day, professional print biographer by night—paid by the word to produce a cascade of political and poetic lives, from British statesmen to writers such as Oliver Goldsmith and Jonathan Swift. Forster's biographical career culminated in his monumental life of Charles Dickens (1872). For this print biography Forster was paid the sum of 10 shillings and 6 pence *per page*, his contract requiring "not less than 600 pages per annum"—a guaranteed annual income of £315.[15]

Market-driven by a society obsessed with reputation, such biographers were sucked into a Victorian vortex where veneration was extolled, but criticism of a man's private life and, above all, good name threatened to tarnish the whole Victorian edifice of work, empire, and medals. When Forster did in fact dare to indicate aspects of Dickens' life that were deemed unpalatable to middle-class sensibilities (such as Dickens' treatment of his first wife), he was excoriated. In his previous biographical compilations, he had indulged in hero-worship that accorded with the Victorian ideal, and had located the secret of popularity by commemorating men of achievement who overcame difficult odds. In Dickens, whom he had known as an intimate colleague, he did so too—but he also dared to expose the psychic, even physical costs of such a Victorian success story, expressed in novelist's hubris, nervous breakdowns, and marital messes. Such truth-telling resulted in widespread condemnation not of Dickens (who was a literary hero) but of the biographer.

Novelist Mary Ann Evans—who as "George Eliot" was living adulterously with a married man—deplored, with others, the fact that, in quoting so many of Dickens' letters and documents and exposing Dickens' private life to public view, Forster's biography was "stuffed with criticism and other matter which would be better in limbo"—that is, left to writers of *fictional* biography like herself.[16]

Interestingly, Eliot had translated a biography, a German life of Jesus, as her first major publication.[17] As an aspiring novelist, however, she saw *fiction,* not nonfiction, as the proper vehicle for *intimate* life depiction; intimacy, in public hands, could breed contempt. Evans knew that, as a "fallen woman" living in "sin," she could never have achieved her reputation as a great novelist in Victorian Britain had her alias been exposed. Understandably, she wanted to keep her cover.

This was, indeed, the point, as it affected nineteenth-century biography: *privacy* preserved one's *reputation.* Biographical privacy thus became sacrosanct in Victorian society.

In sum, nonfiction and fiction divided the Victorian literary spoils in relation to the lives of individuals: the one *maintaining* reputations, the other destroying them—but only in make-believe.

Commissioned Portraiture

Forster was not the only victim of the Victorian need for stain-removal. Often the casualties were writers who had the best of intentions, but who misjudged the determination of surviving widows and family to commission a whitewash, not a biography. Some of the most controversial biographical works of the nineteenth century were thus the results of biographical commissions that went awry.

Thomas Jefferson Hogg had been a college friend of the famous English poet Percy Shelley. Hired by Shelley's posthumous (and pompous) daughter-in-law, Jane, Hogg was initially given complete access to the poet's letters and papers. But his first two volumes, completed in 1858, did not please Lady Shelley (whose husband had succeeded to the baronetcy). They amounted, she complained, to a "fantastic caricature" and she would not allow them to go "forth to the public with my sanction." She withdrew access to Shelley's papers, and Hogg was forced to abandon the work that year.[18] The family engaged in cover-ups for decades afterward.

Another commissioned but then contested work was that of James Anthony Froude, who was asked by the great Victorian historian Thomas Carlyle to be his posthumous official biographer. Froude subsequently fell afoul of Carlyle's surviving daughter, Mary, who considered his four-volume biography (beginning in 1884) to be defamatory—even though Froude had nobly omitted much telling evidence of spousal abuse and impotence. There followed a three-decade-long war between the party of the official biographer and the daughter—one that was never resolved.

In the graphic and plastic arts, a similar tightrope walk characterized commissioned portraiture. The story of

Auguste Rodin's commission to create a statue of Honoré de Balzac is especially revealing. Rodin received the commission in 1891 from the Société des Gens de Lettres (French Society of Literature). After studying many of Balzac's novels as well as print biographies of the writer, and having executed about fifty preparatory studies, Rodin decided to portray Balzac as if standing in the nude, huge and haunted beneath his legendary cloak. The resultant sculpture, exhibited at the Paris Salon of 1898, scandalized the French middle class. The Société de Gens de Lettres duly rejected the work, protesting that Rodin's treatment of the famous author of *La Comédie humaine* didn't accord with the Victorian formula for aggrandizing and polishing the subject. The lack of a finished, shiny surface, so important in academic sculptural style, was considered particularly egregious. Cast in bronze years later, it nevertheless came to be considered one of the greatest examples of biographical sculpture in Western history—long after its creator's death.

Biography's Mealy Mouth

Given the sensitivities of surviving family members and friends, and the money to be made by writing about virtue rather than vice, Victorian biographers—especially those who made their professional living by their output—

mostly chose the easy option. The man the Shelley family ultimately appointed as official biographer of the poet was thus heard to remark that the commission was akin to the "offer of a Bishopric."[19] (A century later, ironically, the *lack* of critical and sexual revelations would doom any biography of a major figure.)

With their bread and butter depending on it, even those professional Victorian biographers who recognized the inherent hypocrisy of their trade toed the line, on both sides of the Atlantic. Few British or American print biographies ever advanced beyond the bounds of decorum, or savaged a man's reputation—and to discourage them further, widows and heirs either guarded posthumous papers zealously, or burned them lest they fall into the "wrong" hands. The widow of the explorer Sir Richard Burton, for example, incinerated all the records of his "research" in the brothels of the Middle East, and John Forster himself burned all but fifty-five of the nearly one thousand letters he possessed from Dickens as "too private"[20]—a situation wonderfully represented in Henry James's novel *The Aspern Papers* (1888), which was based on the real-life saga of the Shelley papers.[21]

To compensate for their somewhat mercenary task as choristers, singing the praises of successful men, professional biographers packed their biographical work with

—⁂—

Edith Henrietta Fowler Hamilton (who married a vicar and became a novelist) recalls the spotless Victorian marriage of her father, solicitor, mayor of Wolverhampton, and a Member of Parliament:

On the 6th October 1857, at St. Mark's Church, Wolverhampton, Henry Hartley Fowler and Ellen Thorneycroft were made man and wife, and from that day the sunshine of domestic happiness began to ripen and mature a character, which from his earliest youth had been subject to a Spartan strictness, and which, owing to disappointments, difficulties and injustices, might have hardened into a depressed and morbid mold. To touch upon the perfectness of their married union with truth, and yet good taste, seems almost impossible for any biographer, much more one for whom it is so noble a heritage and so sweet and sacred a memory.

> Edith Fowler, *The Life of Henry Hartley Fowler, First Viscount Wolverhampton, G.C.S.I.* [Grand Commander of the Star of India] (London: Hutchinson, 1912), p. 40.

—⁂—

"useful" information that had a moral purpose, in the Plutarchian tradition—deliberately or unconsciously using facts and sterling human examples to purvey a Victorian instructional and moral agenda. As Samuel Smiles noted in his biography of George Stephenson, the great engineer urged his students to "educate themselves" and to "acquire that habit of self-thinking and self-reliance which is the spring of all true manly actions."[22] Such biographies were, as Smiles put it, "almost equivalent to Gospels, teaching high living, high thinking, and energetic action for their own and the world's good."[23] Rarely, if ever, did such documentary biographers step over the boundaries of convention either in artistic or structural terms, let alone reveal the intimate private life and psychological travails of their subjects. *Lives of Distinguished Shoemakers* (1849), *Heroes of Industry* (1866), *Lives of the Electricians* (1887, two volumes), *Heroes of the Telegraph* (1891) . . . There was no letup. "How delicate, how decent is English biography," Carlyle—prolific historian and biographer himself—once remarked proudly. "Bless its mealy mouth!"[24]

CHAPTER 5

The Early Twentieth Century

*E*volution proceeds as a struggle of survival and mutation against invading pathogens and environmental pressures—indeed, humans are often depicted by evolutionary biologists as similar to Lewis Carroll's Red Queen: constantly running just to be able to stay in the same place.

Certainly the Victorian era's writers of biographies, authors of biographical plays, and painters and sculptors of portraits, for all their energy, industry, and moral conviction, did not run hard enough or fast enough. It's true that many of them—like the editors of the *Dictionary of National Biography* (Sir Leslie Stephen and his successor, Sir Sidney Lee)—were, at the very least, assured of a knighthood for their services, or even a peerage, as in the case of Gladstone's print biographer, Lord Morley, and that of the top Victorian portrait painter, Lord Leighton. Yet such a supine approach to Johnson's great challenge did not prepare documentary biographies for the inevitable attack by pathogens from outside the realm of biography—or, eventually, from within.

Burning the evidence, as Lady Byron did with her husband's memoirs, was no longer enough. Biography's well-fed, well-remunerated, and always submissive, fawning/glorifying form had become too wooden, too complacent, too unimaginative to defend itself from attack or to develop its potential. The very mediocrity of its practitioners, too, made it vulnerable. "The popular idea," writer Edmund Gosse observed in 1901, "seems to be that no one is too great a fool, or too complete an amateur, or too thoroughly ignorant of composition, to undertake 'the life' of an eminent person."[1]

Thus, as the new century dawned, artists and scientists working in fields *other* than written biography began to covet the very thing that was the mainstay and rationale of biography: *real* lives, with their inexhaustible content of real-life *experiences,* especially personal and private ones.

Among the first, covetous, would-be colonizers of print biography in the new century was a Viennese neurologist, who for some years, in his Bergstrasse apartment, had been writing up medical case histories rather in the manner of Arthur Conan Doyle: Sherlock Holmesian life stories such as *Anna O., The Rat Man,* and *Dora* (and later, most famously, *The Wolf Man*). This learned physician was Sigmund Freud.

Forbidden Fruit

As Freud recognized, the depiction of real lives was hobbled by the failure of print biographers to call a spade a spade. Manet's *Déjeuner sur l'Herbe* of 1868 had pictured it all perfectly: fully clothed Victorian men picnicking on the grass around a completely nude woman, who, for her part, could be shown in her frank, voluptuous, intimate nakedness, staring challengingly at the painter amid her cast-off garments. The disparity was permissible thanks to the fine-arts tradition of the nude, which went back to classical times. This chink in the policing of public art dictated that a statue of a *real* individual must be clothed, but an anonymous or fictive individual could be portrayed stark naked.

This boundary between fiction and nonfiction, whether in print or on canvas, remained strictly enforced in Victorian society. Thus, when John Singer Sargent dared in 1884 to paint the portrait of a recognizable, somewhat risqué society lady posing with the strap of her gown slipping off her naked shoulder, and then titled it *Portrait of Madame X* instead of, say, *Medea,* the picture had to be withdrawn from public view. Sargent duly repainted it with the strap in its proper place, but the damage was done—and the portrait was not exhibited again until the twentieth century.[2]

Freud had no such qualms, and he was unwilling to paint his clients with any shoulder-straps at all. Following Sargent's initial example, he published his first pseudonymous case study, *Dora* (originally titled *Fragment of an Analysis of a Case of Hysteria*), in 1905, using medicine's white-coated professional license rather than the license of a portrait painter—though even Freud, like Manet, knew he was skating on thin ice and might well end up in a *salon des refusés.* A born challenger, he had no illusions. Defying the hypocrisy of his sex-obsessed male colleagues (includ-

---

12. Nudity, or semi-nudity, was acceptable in Victorian art as beauty, so long as the model remained anonymous. John Singer Sargent's *Portrait of Madame X,* however, fooled no one: its subject was easily recognizable as Virginie Avegno, the New Orleans–born wife of French banker Pierre Gautreau. The oil painting, in which her gown strap was shown slipping down her shoulder, had to be withdrawn from exhibition in Paris in 1884 for offending public morals. Reproduced here is a preliminary watercolor painted in 1883. *Fogg Art Museum, Harvard University Art Museums, Bequest of Grenville L. Winthrop, 1943.316; copyright © 2006 President and Fellows of Harvard University.*

ing the novelist and playwright Dr. Arthur Schnitzler), he noted, in his discussion of Dora: "I am aware that—in this city at least—there are many physicians who (revolting though it may seem) choose to read a case history of this kind not as a contribution to the psychopathology of the neuroses, but as a *roman à clef* designed for their private delectation."[3]

Such hypocrisy was, Freud recognized, typical of Viennese imperial society: a culture in which numerous artistic works (such as Schnitzler's banned 1896 play *Reigen*, or *La Ronde*) danced around the forbidden, intimate topic of sex—which, thanks to Victorian prudery, thereby acquired even greater erotic attraction. As Michel Foucault would later observe, the very uptightness and obfuscation that characterized Victorian and indeed much pre-Victorian society created a tantalizing zone "if not of utter silence, at least of tact and discretion: between parents and children, for instance, or teachers and pupils, or masters and domestic servants." The underlying emotions were ripe for Freud's unmasking—though, as Foucault showed, Freud often removed the wrong disguise (as he did in misdiagnosing Dora, who, far from being "in love with Herr K," was a lesbian who had shared a bed with Herr K's wife).[4]

Undeterred, Freud resolved to bring the walls of biography's Jericho tumbling down with his new psychoanalytic trumpet—the better to expose the would-be strumpet. "Now, in this case history," Freud declared of Dora (real name Ida Bauer), "sexual questions will be discussed with all possible frankness, the organs and functions of sexual life will be called by their proper names, and the pure-minded reader can convince himself from my description that I have not hesitated to converse upon such subjects in such language even with a young woman."[5]

Encouraged by his own shocking success, if not with patients (Dora had broken off Freud's treatment of her hysteria), then with his pioneering medical psycho-biographies of them, Freud decided to go further. In 1909 he penned for the weekly meeting of his loyal coterie, the Viennese Psychoanalytic Society, a pioneering study of a man he'd never met, save *through* a biography: Leonardo da Vinci.

"The Domain of Biography Must Become Ours"

Freud's arrogance, in terms of biography, was spellbinding. Convinced he'd cracked the code of life analysis, past as well as present, Freud began to envision a new age and a new colonial empire of psychoanalysis—one that would celebrate itself, in its first foray outside the realm of scientific medicine, with the conquest of life depiction, or biography: reaching into those areas long considered taboo, the true "forme internall," whose manifold, wily psychological dissimulations would henceforth be explored not only by biographical escapees such as Dostoyevsky, using quasi-real life stories to entertain and enlighten through fiction, but also by trained doctor-analysts.

In a private letter to his Swiss protégé C. G. Jung, with completely unselfconscious hubris, Freud confided that "the domain of biography, too, must become ours."

It was a historic declaration. And to show the way it was to be done, he sent Jung an advance copy of his own secret weapon to defeat the mealy-mouthers: a revolutionary portrait of the greatest artist of the Renaissance, whom he now intended, in a period of rabid homophobia throughout Europe, to "out."

The First Step in Biography

Nineteenth-century novelists such as Gustave Flaubert and Fyodor Dostoyevsky had fearlessly exposed the human capacity for self-deception. Reading a tedious yet fascinating new German biography of Leonardo by Magnus Herzfeld, Freud (who loved Dostoyevsky's work) had realized why conventional biography was failing to provide the same human insight that fictional writers were offering. A real human life should, Freud felt, be considered not as an idealized Victorian exemplar but as a psychological *riddle*. The

solving of that riddle, using the technique of psychoanalysis, would, he told Jung, his heir-apparent, be "the first step
in biography."[6]

Freud was sure that the riddle of Leonardo da Vinci
could easily be unraveled—for in reading Herzfeld's biography, he had been reminded of a "neurotic" patient who
had had a dream much like one Leonardo described in his
notebooks, recently published in facsimile: a daydream in
which, according to Leonardo, a vulture "came down to
me and opened my mouth with its tail, and struck me
many times with its tail against my lip."

Clearly—to Freud—the dream represented fellatio.

Freud's biographical assertions, published in 1910 as *Leonardo da Vinci and a Memory of His Childhood,* deliberately
scandalized middle- and upper-class Viennese "respectable
society," in which oral sex, as Freud admitted, was considered "a loathsome perversion." In his new biography, he
nevertheless repeatedly claimed that the desire to indulge
in such sexual activity was to be found not only among homosexual men in the modern Austro-Hungarian Empire,
but "with great frequency among women today."[7] This
did not stop him from equating fellatio-desire among men
with homosexuality.

In elegant prose (Freud considered his study of Leonardo to be a *Halbdichtung,* or half-fiction, indeed the "only

beautiful thing I have ever written"),[8] the father of psychoanalysis begged his readers not to submit to "indignation"
at what would seem an "unpardonable aspersion on the
memory of a great and pure man." Victorian biographers
were, he claimed, for the most part suffering from idealiza-
tion-fixation problems. "In many ways they have chosen
their hero as the subject of their studies because—for reasons of their personal emotional life—they have felt a special affection for him from the very first. They then devote
their energies to a task of idealization, aimed at enrolling
the great man among the class of their infantile models—
at reviving in him, perhaps, the child's idea of his father."
As a result, they "tolerate in him no vestige of human
weakness or imperfection." Freud warned that in this way
they sacrificed "truth to an illusion, and for the sake of
their infantile phantasies abandon the opportunity of penetrating the most fascinating secrets of human nature."[9]

The Siege Begins

Victorian nonfictional portraiture, whether in print or in
paint, had had it coming, one might say—though unlike
Raleigh's executioner, Freud used a woefully blunt ax on
poor Leonardo's posthumous head, leaving a terrible gash.

Leonardo's reputation never quite recovered from the
blow. Soon his masterpiece, the *Mona Lisa,* was adorned

with a mustache and goatee in a travesty by Marcel Duchamp; the painting itself was stolen from the Louvre and
not recovered for several years. The art critic and connois-
seur Bernard Berenson not only downgraded his assess-
ment of Leonardo, but declared that if the *Mona Lisa* was
never recovered, it would be no great loss.[10] Reputations,
clearly, could be dented, if not ruined, by critical psychoanalytic biography—ample reason, if the Victorians needed
any, for their reluctance to loosen the bounds of conventional biography.

Freud's bloodletting proved disastrous to his larger aim
of colonizing biography as a province of psychology. It so
outraged readers of biography that it brought down an immediate portcullis, behind which the purveyors and consumers of conventional, reputation-enhancing biography
armed themselves. Biographical "infantilists" and fixators
then counterattacked by pointing out that the doctor had
got his *facts* wrong. The vulture in Leonardo's dream, for
example, was not a vulture at all but a kite—whose conno-
tations in Egyptian cultural history (where the vulture, a
mother symbol, is impregnated by the wind) are quite different from those trotted out by the would-be Cortez of
biography. Moreover, besides Leonardo's being brought to
trial for sodomy (though not convicted) early in his career;
besides his never taking a wife; besides his worshiping an

*Freud's outing of one of the greatest artists and inventors
of the Renaissance, Leonardo da Vinci, rested on a psychoanalytic reading of a coded childhood fantasy of fellatio:*

What the phantasy conceals is merely a reminiscence
of sucking—of being suckled—at his mother's breast,
a scene of human beauty that he, like so many artists,
undertook to depict with his brush, in the guise of the
mother of God and her child. There is indeed another
point which we do not yet understand and which we
must not lose sight of: this reminiscence, which has
the same importance for both sexes, has been transformed by the man Leonardo into a passive homosex-

ideal of motherhood; and besides his keeping a coterie of
young male apprentices all his working life, what *proof*
did Freud have to make such a scandalous assertion, they
asked? It was not enough for a biographer to have speculative insight, they objected: he must obey the *rules* of good
historianship and adduce *facts* if he wished to be a biographer.

In short, in 1910 fellow biographers and the reading pub-

ual phantasy. For the time being we shall put aside the question of what there may be to connect homosexuality with sucking at the mother's breast, merely recalling that tradition does in fact represent Leonardo as a man with homosexual feelings. In this connection, it is irrelevant to our purpose whether the charge brought against the young Leonardo was justified or not. What decides whether we describe someone as an invert is not his actual behaviour, but his emotional attitude.

Sigmund Freud, *Leonardo da Vinci and a Memory of His Childhood* (1910), trans. Alan Tyson (New York: W. W. Norton, 1964), p. 38.

lic—though they downgraded Leonardo's posthumous reputation—were not amused.

Father and Son

One biographical work that Freud would possibly have approved, had he read it before savaging biographical "infantilists," was Edmund Gosse's *Father and Son* (1907).

Gosse's first, idealized portrait of his father, *The Life of*

Philip Henry Gosse, FRS, had been published in 1890. In contrast, the revised version, published seventeen years later as *Father and Son: A Study of Two Temperaments,* was so unidealized that Gosse published it anonymously. Friends of Gosse who had heard his private confidences about his father—a distinguished English geologist and naturalist, but a devout member of the Plymouth Brethren—had finally persuaded him to tell the truth. The result was psychological patricide.

Father and Son stood Saint Augustine's *Confessions* on its head—indeed, followed a path directly opposite to that of the Manichean apostate. Whereas Saint Augustine had produced a masterpiece of intellectual autobiography, detailing his path *to* Christian faith, Gosse produced a masterpiece of personally observed, subversive journeying *from* the Christian faith—repainting in the kindest yet firmest prose his august but fanatically faith-filled father as an abu-

---

13. Psychobiography got off to a scandalous start when Sigmund Freud "outed" Leonardo da Vinci as a homosexual in a 1910 biography. Dadaists felt empowered to poke fun at the great artist's reputation. Here Marcel Duchamp's mocking 1919 postcard (a "rectified readymade") travesties the *Mona Lisa* with a mustache and goatee. The image is reproduced from a later lithograph. *Copyright © Collegio Angelo Calmarini, Milan / Bridgeman Art Library / 2006 Artists Rights Society (ARS), New York / ADAGP, Paris / Succession Marcel Duchamp.*

sive religious tyrant. Well reviewed in England, it was in America that Gosse's tale of parental abuse was most rapturously received, for it was in America that writers were preparing to take up the magic baton of autobiography—and thus by extension biography—in a wholly revolutionary way. Gosse's account would, in time, spawn an entire century of revelatory confessions—climaxing in the 1990s with the memoirs of virtually an entire generation of abused children who felt finally empowered to expose their unchecked, indeed church-sanctioned pedophile abuse by Catholic priests in America and elsewhere. Following these books, early in the twenty-first century, came autobiographical confessions so vivid and representative of the human heart that observers wondered if they were, in fact, fact.

All this, however, was far in the future as Freud's brief bid for literary *Lebensraum,* the colonization of biography as a branch of psychoanalysis, was launched, and failed.

The Great War

In other areas of art and scientific inquiry, Freud's ideas were often enthusiastically received—especially in America, where in 1909 Freud had been invited to lecture at Clark University. Moreover, within the traditional field of biography many writers, painters, and sculptors were now chafing at the bit, irked by society's taboos against private and sexual revelations. John Morley's idealization of Prime Minister Gladstone in a three-volume Victorian biography had helped to earn the author a seat in the House of Lords. The accolades did not last long. Writing in 1911, the year after Freud's challenge and still in Morley's lifetime, the novelist and futurist H. G. Wells spoke on behalf of a new generation when he declared Victorian biographies "so unsatisfactory, so untruthful," perpetuating "the worst kind of falsehood—the falsehood of omission. Think what an abounding, astonishing person Gladstone must have been in life, and consider Lord Morley's *Life of Gladstone*, cold, dignified—not a life at all, indeed, so much as embalmed remains; the fire gone, the passions gone, the bowels carefully removed."[11]

That same year, Thomas Mann penned an extraordinarily symbolic novella of Europe sliding toward ruin: *Death in Venice*. In August 1914 his prophecy was fulfilled. Far from being over by Christmas, World War I engulfed the globe—with European armies locked in military stalemate. The noble ideals of patriotism and a cleansing of the national soul through glorious bloodletting (Field Marshal Douglas Haig claimed it was worth sacrificing 10 percent of Britain's young men to ensure the survival of only the nation's fittest) began to wear very thin, as battle after battle—Ypres, Verdun, the Somme, Passchendaele, the Lys, Chemin des Dames—consumed the flower of Europe's manhood, leaving nothing but gnarled vines in the vineyard.

Such carnage proved a monument not to human courage, but to man's industrialized inhumanity. As General Erich Ludendorff launched his final spring offensive on the Western Front in the spring of 1918, however, an even more subversive biography than that of Freud's small Leonardo outrage appeared in print. This time the attack came from *within* the biographical domain—the product of an essayist and stylist of the John Aubrey ilk, not a doctor-psychoanalyst.

Eminent Victorians

Commissioned initially to produce chapters on nine exemplary Victorian lives as a biographical compendium, the young homosexual, would-be writer, and literary aesthete Lytton Strachey had procrastinated for several years, until the drums of war made him half crazy. He became a conscientious objector, incensed at the mounting waste of the lives of young men sent off to battle by white-haired Victorian "heroes." Whittling down his biographical subjects to four, Strachey subjected them not to Freud's penetrating psychoanalysis but, after careful secondary research, to a sort of subtle camp mockery, one by one knocking his targets off their pedestals: ambitious Cardinal Manning, dotty Florence Nightingale, the mad General Charles Gordon of Khartoum, and the sinister Dr. Thomas Arnold, headmaster of Rugby School for boys.

Print biography, Strachey seemed to say, would never be mealy-mouthed again—and after *Eminent Victorians,* it wasn't. Reprinted again and again in 1918, and an instant success on both sides of the Atlantic, *Eminent Victorians* employed—as Thomas Mann would in the field of fiction—the new weapon of irony.

"The End of Gordon" was perhaps Strachey's most brilliant chapter. It took a legendary British hero and put him under a twentieth-century microscope. What Strachey exposed was a religious madman who never married and who was the dupe of Victorian right-wing imperialists hungry for power and empire. Gordon was "by nature farouche," Strachey wrote; "his soul revolted against dinner-parties and stiff shirts, and the presence of ladies—especially of fashionable ladies—filled him with uneasiness. He had, besides, a deeper dread of the world's contaminations." During six years as forts supervisor at Gravesend, at the mouth of the Thames, Colonel Gordon, the hero of great battles in China, was "soon a familiar sight" among the poor. "He was particularly fond of boys," Strachey

Lytton Strachey's famous chronicle of Henry Edward Manning's abandonment of Anglican holy orders, and rise to cardinal's rank in the Roman Catholic church, implied a stinging disbelief in Manning's sincerity. It ended:

The funeral was the occasion of a popular demonstration such as has rarely been witnessed in the streets of London. The route of the procession was lined by vast crowds of working people, whose imaginations, in some instinctive manner, had been touched. Many who had hardly seen him declared that in Cardinal Manning they had lost their best friend. Was it the magnetic vigour of the dead man's spirit that moved them? . . . Or was it, perhaps, the mysterious glamour lingering about him of the antique organization of

added. "Ragged street arabs and rough sailor-lads crowded about him. They were made free of his house and garden; they visited him in the evenings for lessons and advice; he helped them, found them employment, corresponded with them when they went out into the world. . . . Except for his boys and his paupers, he lived alone." Driven by reli-

Rome? For whatever cause, the minds of people had been impressed; and yet, after all, the impression was more acute than lasting. The Cardinal's memory is a dim thing today. And he who descends into the crypt of that Cathedral which Manning never lived to see, will observe, in the quiet niche with the sepulchral monument, that the dust lies thick on the strange, the incongruous, the almost impossible object which, with its elaborations of dependent tassels, hangs down from the dim vault like some forlorn and forgotten trophy—the Hat.

Lytton Strachey, *Eminent Victorians* (London: Penguin, 1986; orig. pub. 1918), p. 108.

gious zeal, Strachey's Gordon saw life as a struggle between the ethereal soul and the corrupt body. Following the promises of one and the curses of the other, man "sees he is not of this world," Gordon had written to his sister; "for when he speaks of himself he quite disregards the body his soul lives in, which is earthly."[12]

14. The devastating irony of Lytton Strachey's *Eminent Victorians* (1918)
marked a new departure in literary biography, mocking four representative Victorian grandees. Here, Henry Lamb's 1914 oil painting depicts the Edwardian aesthete and writer as he begins work
on his masterpiece. The portrait is now in the Fitzwilliam Museum, Cambridge, U.K. *Copyright © Bridgeman Art Library; Estate of
Henry Lamb, reproduced by kind permission of Mrs. Henrietta Phipps.*

As Strachey saw it, General Gordon's fate was to be the sacrificial lamb of Victorian expansionists—an end that Strachey chronicled with painstaking, remorseless objectivity, refusing to be seduced by patriotic cant. After the British retaking of Khartoum, following Gordon's death, a service of remembrance for General Gordon was held, complete with four chaplains from different Christian denominations, and Sudanese buglers. "Every one agreed that General Gordon himself had been avenged, at last. Who could doubt it? General Gordon himself, possibly, fluttering, in some remote Nirvana, the pages of a phantasmal Bible, might have ventured a satirical remark. But General Gordon had always been a contradictious person—even a little off his head, perhaps, though a hero; and besides, he was no longer there to contradict. . . . At any rate, it had all ended very happily—in a glorious slaughter of 20,000 Arabs, a vast addition to the British Empire, and a step in the Peerage for [the architect of the Khartoum imbroglio] Sir Evelyn Baring."[13]

Grief

Though brilliantly effective in smashing Victorian reputations, Strachey's mocking style as a biographer gave little evidence that—attached as he was to his own armchair comfort as a writer rather than a researcher—he could

do any better than his Victorian predecessors in more serious, less sniper-like life depiction; and in rechronicling
the lives of Queen Victoria (1921) and Queen Elizabeth
(1928), Strachey didn't. Nor did others who attempted the
Stracheyan approach. Irony might win Mann the Nobel
Prize (for his novel *The Magic Mountain*), but as a perma-
nent filter it proved a dead end for biography.

Nevertheless, the damage to Victorian hypocrisy, at least,
was done: Strachey's sardonic tone, applied not just to one
but to a representative group of Victorian worthies, punc-
tured the self-satisfied, preening tomes of Victorian hero-
worship. To be sure, a statue was raised near 10 Downing
Street to the "Butcher of the Somme," Field Marshal Haig,
and a fortune was awarded to him from taxpayers' money
for "winning" the supposed "War to End All Wars." But
the Field Marshal's fame and reputation were short-lived.
He had been responsible for millions of casualties and
deaths, their names recorded on small memorials in every
English village and hamlet.

As the price of "victory" was counted, commemoration
became not veneration, in the Victorian tradition, but collective grief, resentment, and uncertainty about the future.
Open revolution might be avoided in Britain and America,
but in both countries "book-length debunking of reputations became a literary fad," as Richard Altick would re-

cord in his history of British and American literary biography. What ensued was a veritable "biography boom" in which "brightly written, studiously irreverent biographies by the hundreds competed on the best-seller lists."[14]

Genius in Life, not Work

Grief makes people turn inward—and in the aftermath of the Great War, biographers for the most part turned away from achievement to explore personality and—in an era finally witnessing the emancipation of women in the West—gender and sexuality. As Gamaliel Bradford noted of the "new biography" in 1929, "Instead of trying to write a man's eulogy, or commemorate his achievements, or hold him up as a profitable example, we are simply trying to understand what manner of man he was, to analyze his character and motives, and to classify him and put him in his place with other groups of human beings." But *how*, given Western society's continuing laws against sodomy (laws that had been reemphasized in Britain in 1886 in a draconian new parliamentary statute against homosexual relations), could this new, post–World War I understanding be expressed in biographical work that was subject to laws governing libel, pornography, and homosexuality— laws and marketplace rules which (as we will see in the case of film, especially) forbade mention of "inversion"?

Oscar Wilde's famous indictment and imprisonment still served as a dire warning to any Briton who advertised his "invert" predilections. Wilde's "hideously, atrociously dramatic, and really interesting" life story had filled the American novelist and failed playwright Henry James, for example, with fascination—and contempt. A repressed homosexual, James had despised Wilde not only for his thespian popularity ("so bad, so clumsy, feeble and vulgar"), but also for his openly gay conduct in the early 1890s ("a fatuous fool, tenth-rate cad," "an unclean beast," "an unspeakable animal").[15] James's own attempt at theater, *Guy Domville,* had proven a disastrous flop; he therefore gloried in Wilde's downfall, which was accomplished in three terrible trials in 1895—trials that had led inexorably to Wilde's conviction for "gross indecency" and his sentencing to two years' imprisonment with hard labor.

Wilde—who died in 1900, soon after his release from prison—had memorably claimed that his "genius" was to be found not in his work, but in his *life.* (His writings, he remarked, showed merely his "talent.") But if Wilde's life was literally *sub judice,* how were biographers to tackle the real personality (and sexuality) rather than the achievement of such an individual? The answer was they couldn't. As Lytton Strachey wrote prophetically to his friend John Maynard Keynes, "Our time will come about a hundred years hence, when preparation will have been made, and compromises come to, so that, at the publication of our letters, everyone will be, finally, converted."[16] But not before.

Goodbye to All That

Strachey's prediction proved not far wrong—indeed, as we shall see, it would eventually be the highly combustible chemical of suppressed human sexuality that, liberated at last, would refuel biographical curiosity and output in the final decades of the twentieth century. In the meantime, however, critical documentary or nonfictional book-biography remained at an impasse, its authors not daring to go beyond Strachey's ironic lens in attacking reputations, lest they fall foul of censors, lord chamberlains, lawyers, and judges.

Chained by centuries-old laws of libel and pornography, as well as by decorum, biographers in the remaining Western democracies had to make do with a kind of indirect speech—a deliberate debunking of myths, rules, and Victorian pomposity that nevertheless masked their failure to tackle the very real life they claimed to want to depict. Thus, for example, Robert Graves penned *Goodbye to All That* (1929), an autobiography in which he gave a first-hand account of what the war had *really* been like in the mud of

Flanders. The book was a sensational success, excoriating, as Strachey had, the stupidity of Britain's leaders, while giving a personal account of the horrors that only a veteran could know. Unlike Strachey, Graves had not been a conscientious objector—in fact, he had been one of the first to join up as an infantry subaltern in the summer of 1914. What he'd then witnessed was the hierarchical class bankruptcy of his own English society, which he painted with devastating honesty, as it sent its young into battle—a fiasco characterized by military idiocy, callousness, mechanized slaughter, and human degradation. His book was one of a series of exposés of the British establishment that made the endless encomia and financial grants to wartime generals seem pathetically unwarranted.

What Graves was unable to tell was the true story of his own personality—which could only be hinted at in a mysterious Afterword to the 1929 edition. The "That" of his goodbye turned out to be (when deciphered and revealed by Richard Perceval Graves sixty years later) the traumatic breakdown of his marriage following a *ménage à quatre* (even a *ménage à cinque* at one point), the attempted suicide of his American mistress, and his determination to run away with her as his muse.[17]

The fact was that—in this strange postwar world, where

the kings had departed only to be replaced by economic, political, and social uncertainty—biography was at a crossroads. As the New York stock market crashed in 1929, and the Western world faced economic depression on a hitherto unimaginable scale, Graves was doubtless right to withhold his most intimate life experiences from his autobiography, in order to return to poetry and historical novels, living in exile with Laura Riding. Nevertheless, the careers of both Strachey and Graves illustrate the death rattle of print biography, like that of parliamentary democracy, by the early 1930s. Certainly no "big" biographers comparable to the Lockharts, Forsters, Morleys, Partons, and Stephenses of the nineteenth century came forward; and this vacuum was filled by a tribe of frustrated amateurs, American academics, and journeymen of letters such as Hesketh Pearson, André Maurois, Hugh Kingsmill, Irving Stone, Harold Nicolson, and Philip Guedalla. These writers represented a genre that was commercially successful but that had clearly exceeded its sell-by date.

Quo Vadis?

Both André Maurois and Harold Nicolson declared in the late 1920s that print biographers *must* respond to the impulses and needs of modern times if print biography was to adapt and survive. *Quo vadis,* however? After thousands of years of human life depiction, the *Oxford English Dictionary* definition of "biography" still confined the once multimedia effort at recording real life to the mere "history of the lives of individual men, as a branch of literature." In the aftermath of World War I, such a complacent lexicographic definition seemed, to modernist artists, as outdated as the medium of print biography itself. *Women,* for a start, would have to be included in any new definition of biography. Moreover, movements such as Post-Impressionism, Expressionism, Futurism, Imagism, Vorticism, Dadaism, and Surrealism had, in tune with new psychology, turned traditional views of art and portraiture upside down, so that it was clear lexicographers would have to expand the purview of "biography" to include not only female lives but interior personae and sexuality. The biographer's *own* life would have to be acknowledged as a crucial lens—whether expressed in photography, film, radio, or, finally, sound movies. In sum, the notion of biography as a pursuit limited to a "branch of literature" would *have* to be redefined and enlarged to embrace more genders, new genres, and more media. But if its express purpose was now the delineation of personality rather than achievement, how could this aim be fulfilled in societies that still forbade the necessary frankness?

A Struggle for the Soul of Biography

On pain of imprisonment with hard labor, Strachey remained, to the end of his life (he died in 1932), unable to write about his own real world: the world of Bloomsbury and a group of artists and academics who accepted his and often their own homosexuality, and refused to denounce or expose him. Likewise, Graves felt it ethically right to expose the reality of modern war on the Western Front, but wrong to reveal the private torment he was going through with his *ménage à quatre* in West London—scandal that would have embarrassed his parents, hurt his wife, and harmed his children. Yet how long could such intimate details of real lives be withheld, in a culture whose social structure was cracking to the point of possible revolution?

The war between the classes was reaching a flashpoint across Europe—as was the war between the sexes, which had taken a further turn in 1929 when women over twenty-one were finally accorded the vote in Britain, a right that British women over thirty had enjoyed since 1918 and that all American women over the age of twenty-one had had since 1920. This cultural upheaval was reflected and represented in ever-proliferating ways by pioneering artists, poets, novelists, psychologists, and sociologists of what was called "modernism." Each explored afresh the human condition, especially with regard to gender and sexuality, as modernist movements swept through art, architecture, sculpture, drama, film, and radio—introducing revolutionary changes in style, content, marketing, and technology. "Art" and professional status protected (for the most part) practitioners ranging from Picasso to Pirandello—but woe betide a real-life depicter who sought to portray people as they actually were.

A Stain on Vanessa's White Dress

One pioneering writer who was deeply vexed by the challenge of modern biography was Virginia Woolf. Daughter of Leslie Stephen, the founding editor of *The Dictionary of National Biography*, Woolf had become one of a number of artistic minds determined to liberate literature from its shackles and introduce a more open discussion of human intimacy.

"Suddenly the door opened and the long sinister figure of Mr. Lytton Strachey stood on the threshold," Woolf later recalled in a talk at the private Memoir Club. His entrance heralded her conversational liberation. Strachey pointed to a stain on the white dress worn by Virginia's sister. "Semen?" he inquired.

"Can one really say it?" Woolf remembered thinking, "and we burst out laughing. With that one word all barriers of reticence and reserve went down. A flood of sacred fluid seemed to overwhelm us. Sex permeated our conversation. The word bugger was never very far from our lips. We discussed copulation with the same excitement and openness that we had discussed the nature of good."[18]

As a director of her own publishing company, the Hogarth Press, Woolf was, however, well aware that obscenity laws would make publication of such a discussion impossible at the time. As she noted in her diary and her correspondence, she had watched with fascination as Strachey made his name as a biographer trashing the biographical approach of her own father; yet however unsavory his conversation, Strachey had found himself unable to write—or at least publish—dirty. Frustrated, Woolf was suddenly seized by an epiphany. It "sprung upon me how I could revolutionise biography in a night," she wrote excitedly to her lover Vita Sackville-West on October 9, 1927; "it's all about you and the lusts of your flesh and the lure of your mind."[19]

The result, the following year, was *Orlando: A Biography,* in which Woolf neatly avoided legal and social indictment by writing a spoof of a life. Orlando's career was stretched to cover some three hundred years—the better to question the biographer's "plodding" notion of time, but also to note changes *in* the times, she claimed. More important,

this method ensured that the hero could become a trans-
sexual: the eponymous hero becoming a "she" as Orlando
changed his clothes and sex halfway through the life story.
If print biography could not batter down the doors of
English decorum and reputation in conventional biography, Woolf had realized, it would have to mask itself in
fictitious portraiture.

Like *Eminent Victorians, Orlando* was well received by a
British and American public tired of the conventions of
biographical writers seeking knighthoods (like Woolf's father) or prizes for gilding the lilies of (usually male) establishment figures. Yet also like *Eminent Victorians,* Woolf's
novel offered no real way forward for print biographers. As
Freud had found when publishing his own chaste Victorian
autobiography in 1924, it was far easier to mock than to replace.[20] However much she might poke fun at its limitations, Woolf was, as a lesbian, as impotent to change the
parameters of biography as the homosexual Strachey. Her
biography of the art critic Roger Fry, published in 1940,
would be widely considered not only the worst book she
ever wrote, but a complete failure as a biography, despite
the fact that she had known him and his circle intimately,
through her sister Vanessa. Concerned not to upset Fry's
widow, or scandalize society, or run into legal difficulties,
she found herself unable to portray the real Fry—a prob-

lem she did not face in her fiction, her private correspondence, or her diary, where she positively reveled in the skewering of personalities and their reputations.[21]

What made Woolf's failure doubly disappointing was that Roger Fry, as an art critic and painter, had been one of the founding fathers of modernism in British art. Graphic portraiture, in particular, was undergoing its most radical shakeup in millennia. Centuries of dignified graphic portraiture had suddenly been exploded in the revolutionary work of a host of modernists. As William Rubin would write, when later inaugurating an exhibition of Picasso's portraits at the Metropolitan Museum of Art, "It was assumed that the *raison d'être* of a portrait was to communicate the appearance and personality of the sitter." However, by defining the portrait as a record of "the artist's personal responses to the subject, Picasso transformed it from a purportedly objective document into a frankly subjective one."[22] It was a modernist torch that had passed from Picasso to Matisse, Kokoschka to Grosz, Kandinsky to Beckmann, Max Ernst to Man Ray, Dalí to Magritte: all contraverting and subverting respectability with their revolutionary approaches to perspective, color, realism, and content. How long, in such circumstances, could print biography, as the written record of real lives, lag behind its peers?

The answer: longer than people expected—and for good reasons.

An Unpublished Kick in the Pants

Whatever their own failings as documentary biographers, both Woolf and Strachey correctly perceived the challenges facing print biography: namely, the problem of revealing, in the 1920s and 1930s, the real and *private* lives of biographical subjects. These were not obstacles easily overcome in a Western society that was still wedded to personal privacy, to Victorian conventions in the discussion of sexuality, and to the sexless portrayal of real lives; indeed, there was general confusion regarding what exactly should replace the moral, uplifting agenda of the Victorians. Sculptors and painters were proposing brilliant solutions, but for nonfiction writers and artists, the way forward was blocked. Adolf Hitler was free to record his life story and the wildest racial myths and theories in *Mein Kampf,* but the struggle to portray honestly the problems of personality—problems of sexuality and identity—remained *verboten* throughout most of the West. Even American autobiographers, traditionally the most courageous in tackling the truth honestly, found it hard to get published outside the émigré presses of Paris. From Anaïs Nin to Henry Miller, American autobiographers sought to defy the rules: deliberately subverting, revising, and redefining the individual human self as they did so, and thereby validating minority/marginal/forbidden identities. As Henry Miller said in the preface to his own intimate life, novelized as *Tropic of Cancer* (1934): "This is not a book. This is a libel, a slander, defamation of character. . . . This is a prolonged insult, a gob of spit in the face of Art, a kick in the pants to God, Man, Destiny, Time, Love, Beauty."[23] But he could not get his work published in either America or Britain (one publisher who did attempt a U.S. edition was sent to prison for ten years in 1940).

Biography was, in sum, stymied.

An Egalitarian Stance

For all its problems, as Virginia Woolf had noted in an essay she published in the *New York Herald Tribune,* biography was nevertheless slowly emerging from its long Victorian night. Society's blinds *were* slowly being raised, especially with regard to sex. Furthermore, biographers were at last beginning to see themselves, in the wake of radical portrait painters, as less subservient than their Victorian predecessors. The attitude of most Victorian biographers had been, as in portraiture, that of a "serious and sympathetic companion," as Woolf put it, "toiling even slavishly in the footsteps of his hero."[24] Following the pioneering work of Picasso, Freud, and Strachey, the biographer was again being encouraged, at least by his more sophisticated audience, to write his portrayal on *egalitarian* terms with the subject. The biographer's stance was thus altered forever. "Whether friend or enemy, admiring or critical," Woolf noted, the biographer "is an equal," demanding "his freedom and his right to independent judgment." Moreover, he had greater liberty to *select* from his source materials. "He chooses; he synthesizes; in short he has ceased to be the chronicler; he has become," Woolf acknowledged, "an artist."[25]

The twentieth-century print biographer might be on the way back to becoming an artist, but what he or she produced was not yet, in Woolf's eyes, art. Speaking as a novelist, she felt biography was produced "at a lower degree of tension" than a work of art of the pure imagination, "and for that reason its creations are not destined for the immortality which the artist now and then achieves for his creations."[26]

Doubtless this was true—at least if one thinks of enduring works of great fictional literature or art, and if biography is held to embrace only written nonfiction. What Woolf did not foresee, however, was a future in which the *dramatization* of real-life stories—even her own, in the print and cinematic versions of Michael Cunningham's *The*

Hours—would create a new *blend* of biography, somewhere between fiction and nonfiction: a blend Woolf thought could never happen without causing the biographer to lose "both worlds."[27] She warned against mixing "the truth of real life and the truth of fiction," a conflation that would mean "they destroy each other. . . . Let it be fact, one feels, or let it be fiction; the imagination will not serve two masters, simultaneously."[28]

Whether Woolf's prediction would prove true or not was impossible to judge in the 1920s. But in the 1930s the matter became critical in a way that Woolf had not foreseen. Just as her own intended thesis on feminism, *Three Guineas,* turned into a tract against fascism and war, so too concern with fact and fiction in biographical work would morph into a far more worrying anxiety: the danger that biography would be applied to real people for political purposes, as *propaganda.* A danger that, ironically, was vastly magnified by the most potentially intimate of all media: film.

CHAPTER 6

The Rise of Film

ilm would, by the end of the twentieth century, transform biography, so a brief survey of its history is in order—especially since, in the 1930s, film became the medium in which the very *raison d'être* of biography was most vividly contested.

From its invention, at the end of the nineteenth century, cinema had proven violent, subversive—and intimate. In his classic account of its emergence, the film historian Charles Musser noted how, through control of its actuality and documentary content, the new medium of cinema was initially intended to appeal to conservative white males: it offered nonfiction films "made by men, primarily for men."[1]

Indeed, the movies did appeal largely to men—especially for their early *erotic* content, such as documentary scenes of female dancers or women *en déshabille*. Nevertheless, this controlling male agenda was quickly swept up into the wider, socially subversive quality of the new medium. Films attracted spectators high and low. Not only was there a new, exponentially expanding social *market*, thanks to the cheap method of reproduction—a market that included equal numbers of women—but the passionate psychological motivations of *filmmakers* soon drove the medium to occupy the "empty corners" of cinema which early documentary filmmakers had ignored, or passed over. "Sex and violence figured prominently in American motion pictures from the outset," Musser writes,[2] tracing film's antecedents back to magic-lantern images, so reminiscent of man's first cave paintings—which had likewise featured violent interactions. After seventeen thousand years, intimate observation of the beasts of nature had been transmuted into observation, simply, of *human* nature.

It is impossible to exaggerate the cultural impact of twentieth-century film. Almost overnight, film became a popular, indeed subversively populist democratic medium; its moving images, as Musser notes, were "consistent with the individualized, peephole nature of the viewing experience: they showed amusements that often offended polite and/or religious Americans."[3]

Early cinema produced a multitude of fictional stories in a sexually licentious vein, beginning with *The Gay Shoe Clerk* (1903), the tale of an employee who steals his thrills by sliding his hand up a customer's proffered leg, only to be rewarded with an umbrella lashing by her chaperone— all captured by the hovering camera for the delight of the audience. As such dramatized excitements captured audience attention, documentary films had found themselves unable to compete, given society's moral rules regarding the depiction of real as opposed to fictionalized life. The increasing marginalization of nonfiction film, Musser observes, was "a defeat for the efforts of traditional cultural arbiters to dictate cultural and ideological tastes," while fictional movies, especially comedies, ridiculed convention; they "promoted more relaxed attitudes towards sex and contributed to the breakdown of Victorian values."[4]

Most of these values were patriarchal. Not only did early film set the stage for women's suffrage in the second decade of the twentieth century, but the new medium permitted women as well as men to become the voyeur, attending to the "usually forbidden world of masculine amusement."[5] Films of famous boxing matches, showing men stripped to the waist, proved especially popular. From now on, no area of human interest was off limits to the prying lens—driven by mass, popular curiosity that had been repressed for hundreds, if not thousands, of years.

Though the lives (as well as deaths) of figures such as Buffalo Bill, Julius Caesar, Cleopatra, Christopher Columbus, Daniel Boone, Saul and David, Jesus of Nazareth, Pope Leo II, Kit Carson, President McKinley, Mary Queen of Scots, Moses, Napoleon, President Theodore Roosevelt, Richard Wagner, George Washington, and Kaiser Wilhelm II all featured in cinema productions before World War I, they were soon completely outnumbered, outclassed, and outwatched by fictional films—a gap that became an immense chasm after the war.

How had such a radical and unexpected reversal happened? Biograph and Vitagraph, two of the most successful early production companies in America, had incorporated the notion of *life* into their very names; likewise Bioscope, an early projector, and Biopticon, a camera/projector. But as cinemas, in their shadowy spaces, increasingly played on human *fantasy* as well as *projection*—literal and metaphorical—rather than true-life documentary, fictional films came to offer a closer, more vivid portrait of human lives. Though film thereby heightened mass curiosity about real people, cinematic biographers found themselves unable for the most part to compete, either because of lingering social conventions (aided by legal protections) concerning privacy, laws governing libel, or simply artists' cowardice. Documentary film production thus remained, at a biographical level, risibly unchallenging in a revolutionary new medium that was daring and subversive at every other level, from optical perception to subject matter.

One exception, however, was Abel Gance's life of the young Corsican artillery officer who became master of Europe: Napoleon Bonaparte.

Napoléon vu par Abel Gance

Abel Gance—born illegitimate (his natural father was a doctor), raised by a mechanic—had made his name at an early age in theater and then branched out into cinema. His silent film *J'accuse,* distributed in 1919, depicted the haunting tragedy of mass slaughter in the trenches during World War I. Gance then directed the mesmerizing film *La Roue* (The Wheel). In a state of despair and psychic uprootedness after his mistress, Ida Danis, and his closest friend, the famous actor Séverin-Mars, died in the 1919 flu epidemic, he became determined to retell, on celluloid, the story of his nation's strongman. The result was *Napoléon vu par Abel Gance* (1927).

In a series of rhythmic black-and-white frames running like streams, eddies, currents, and flooding tides, the biopic was accompanied only by music—composed by Gance himself. He had read more than seventy biographies of the emperor's life, in an attempt to master authentic details. He then set about creating a new kind of cinematic epic using recently invented film techniques, as well as devices such as hand-held cameras, 3-D, and panoramic triple-split screens, which were decades in advance of their time.

Gance's five-hour film, like Freud's outing of Leonardo, was too insistent and too silent. It bombed in the Roaring Twenties—yet it did, as reviewers commented, point up the danger or potential (depending on one's point of view) of biographical film as *artistic propaganda.* Radio was already adding a new mass technology and artistic/informational medium to the business of real life-depiction after World War I; audiences of millions were now able to hear the real voices of emperors and peasants alike. With the advent of the soundtrack in 1928, movies overnight became the hypnotic opium of the people—a medium that could be exploited not only for money, in the style of Hollywood entertainers, but also for political purposes, as first the Russian Communists and then Adolf Hitler quickly recognized.

Ideological Directions

The potential of cinematic biography for political manipulation of the masses had not gone unaddressed in the democracies. Propaganda in all media, from books to posters, had become a seminal weapon in World War I, as important as artillery. But while the lessons were quickly forgotten or viewed as irrelevant during peacetime in the democracies, they were not lost on Lenin, Trotsky, Mussolini, Ataturk, Stalin, Hitler, and other aspiring dictators. Soon a new tide of hero-worship, deliberately fanned by callous apparatchiks, flooded the Soviet Union, Italy, and Germany—once the most conservative country in Europe—whose popularly elected Austrian-born chancellor obtained total power by consent of the Reichstag, as his nation's Führer (leader), in the spring of 1933.

In the Soviet Union the "ideological direction" of production was strictly controlled by the Commissariat of Education—a body whose members, as Marxists, were hostile to the idealization of individuals. Cinematic pioneers therefore reveled in *anti*-biographical depictions of class warfare, such as Sergei Eisenstein's *Strike* and *Battleship Potemkin,* followed by *October* and *The General Line.* The dynamic energy of such films soon fell victim to the suspicions and stranglehold of the Communist Party, which ordered the excision of any "remnants of bourgeois influence"—especially individualism. Biopics in the USSR exemplified the problem. Eisenstein's *Alexander Nevsky* was withdrawn from distribution after the German-Soviet Pact of 1939, and Part II of his *Ivan the Terrible* was detested by Stalin. Eisenstein was eventually denounced by the Central Committee of the Communist Party for having—like Walter Raleigh in his history of princes—"betrayed his ignorance of historical fact by showing the progressive bodyguard of Ivan the Terrible as a degenerate band, rather like the Ku Klux Klan, and Ivan the Terrible himself, who was a strong man of will and character, as weak and indecisive, somewhat like Hamlet."[6]

Hitler, however, was unrepentantly bourgeois—and loved film, with its magical realism. When the beautiful young actress-director Leni Riefenstahl, sensing the importance of the Führer and his Nazi movement to his nation and the world, approached Hitler to congratulate him, he was touched—indeed, she later claimed, he made an almost comically wooden pass at her, which she rejected. Sublimating his feelings, Hitler arranged for Riefenstahl, who was a supporter but not a card-carrying member of the Nazi Party, to make a film of the 1933 Nuremberg National Socialist Party Rally, under the supervision of the military, the Reichswehr.

Impressed by Riefenstahl's documentary, titled *Victory of Faith,* Hitler asked her to make a sequel recording the 1934 rally. When she complained that Nazi Party pressures made mediocrity inevitable, Hitler personally commissioned her to make the film. It became one of the most controversial biographical movies of all time: *Triumph of the Will*—Hitler's will.

Triumph of the Will

Riefenstahl's 1935 paean to Hitler and his charisma was made with a staff of 170 assistants—the largest film team ever to make a documentary. With its lyrical composition, brilliant editing, and skillful use of music, it won adulation in Germany and garnered major national and international prizes. Moreover, it contributed immeasurably to the cult of Germany's new dictator; it has often been called "the most powerful propaganda film ever made."[7] The critic Ken Kelman later extolled Riefenstahl for achieving "the definitive cinematic obliteration of the division between fantasy and 'reality.'"[8]

Like Picasso and the great portraitists of the modernist era, Riefenstahl had stepped beyond the traditional frontiers of objective chronicle to infuse the film with her own

15. The new hagiography: German actress and film director Leni Riefenstahl, photographed while directing *Triumph of the Will,* her award-winning documentary paean to Adolf Hitler as Führer at Nuremberg in 1934, considered the greatest work of film propaganda ever made. *Copyright © The Granger Collection, New York.*

subjective adoration of the Führer. It reflected what Hitler meant for her and for millions of her fellow Germans. The result was spellbinding.

Virginia Woolf, in her essay "The New Biography," had declared that for the biographer "truth of fact and truth of fiction are incompatible."[9] But modernist portrait painters had already proved her wrong by their insistence on subjectively stated truth when depicting a real individual. Harold Nicolson had likewise felt that a strict line must be maintained between the objective reality of the subject and "undue" subjectivity on the part of the author.[10] To his credit, Nicolson had drawn attention to the fact that biographers, if they were to tackle a life imaginatively, had to avoid at least the "impurity" not of sex or vice or even violence, but of an "extraneous theory or conception"—that is, a religious or political agenda—lest biography revert to hagiography.[11]

Nicolson was right to be anxious. Yet what chance did such a purist approach to print biography have, when it came to contesting the new social Darwinism of Fascists, Nazis, and Communists in the 1930s? The truth was that, in an age of dictatorships, when books were being burned like heretics at the stake, the sound-assisted two-dimensional image was becoming perhaps the greatest weapon of mass destruction of the twentieth century: propaganda.

Biography on Trial

It would be nice to be able to say, as a biographer, that the evolutionary response of Western biographers to such a development—which compromised the very life-blood of biography as, in Edmund Gosse's words, "the truthful record of an individual and composed as a work of art"—was immediate, virile, and effective. Sadly, this was not the case. Appeasement and isolationism provided little evidence that democracy (and, with it, "pure" biography) could be saved. Even Hollywood was not spared threats against films critical of Hitler and the Nazis: Joseph P. Kennedy, U.S. Ambassador to Britain and former president of RKO Studios, flew from London to Hollywood in 1940 expressly to warn Jewish producers and directors not to make anti-Nazi or anti-Hitler movies.[12]

Biographical writers and artists had often endured such trials before in Western history, under dictatorships and absolute monarchies, but never on such a scale. Totalitarian regimes were now employing the full range of communications media, in every conceivable form, while democracies clung still to their laws of libel, making criticism of living people impossible. Though Charlie Chaplin made a scathing film satire of Hitler's life, *The Great Dictator,* in 1940, until well after World War II only a single serious, well-researched, critical biography of Hitler appeared in print (Konrad Heiden's *Hitler: A Biography,* published in 1936). Mussolini and Stalin likewise escaped censure.

Democracy, armed with its punitive laws of defamation, seemed unable to defend itself. Critical biographies and autobiographies that *did* appear in the democracies often met with yawns, embarrassment, or commercial failure. Many more simply wound up on lawyers' reject piles: unpublished, unbroadcast, unstaged, unproduced, undistributed.

George Orwell's autobiographical account of his participation in the Spanish Civil War, *Homage to Catalonia* (1938), exposed the autocratic methods of the Soviet Union and its NKVD apparatus, dedicated to ruthlessly exterminating fellow socialists rather than opposing the fascist army of General Franco. Its commissioning publisher, Victor Gollancz, was too scared to issue the book in London, and its eventual English publisher, Secker and Warburg, managed to sell only a few hundred copies in Orwell's lifetime. It was not published at all in the United States until the 1950s.

To be sure, Jews and other opponents of the Nazis protested the showing of Riefenstahl's films *Triumph of the Will* and *Olympia* in New York. But amid the prevailing American mood of isolationism, Hollywood's producers, especially Jewish ones, were simply reluctant to court domestic anti-Semitism by countering Nazi propaganda with Hollywood propaganda. Thus, when the Great White Hope of American stage and cinema—the young actor, radio producer, and dramaturge Orson Welles—decided to show his nation what modern film biography *should* do on behalf of democracy to counter propaganda, he was threatened with libel, the destruction of his master reels, and the blocking of all-important advertising, reviews, and film distribution.

Citizen Kane

Deliberately designed and titled to bring a fictional "great man of history" down to ordinary human size, and aiming to introduce a more critical dimension to cinema, *Citizen Kane* was structured as a biographical research journey made by a team of newspaper reporters to discover the meaning of a media mogul's last word: "Rosebud."

Whereas Virginia Woolf had mocked conventional biography, yet, in *Roger Fry,* had proven unable to provide a better example of how a serious modern print biography might be composed, the twenty-four-year-old Orson Welles first mocked the conventional form of the newsreel obituary, and then presented a bewitching example of how serious modern film-biography *could* be undertaken. He illustrated in his film all the techniques of a professional biographer: archival research, visits to scenes of the life, interviews with surviving witnesses, colleagues, and spouses. In an especially vivid and effective innovation, he took their reminiscences as told to the research team and dramatized them as flashbacks.

This sense of *quest*—of a biographical mystery or inquiry, of investigators peering and peeping behind the curtain of respectability and privacy with which the rich and powerful protect themselves—pervaded the movie from beginning to flaming end, as Kane's beloved childhood sled is consumed by fire.

No biographical play or print biography has ever come close to matching the power, imagination, and technical virtuosity of *Citizen Kane*—nor is there a better graphic illustration of the biographical process of research and inquiry. Unfortunately for Welles, despite all his efforts to dissociate the figure of Kane from any living model, the character's life and career seemed suspiciously close to

---

16. Orson Welles's fictional film biography *Citizen Kane* (1941) was modeled largely on the life of William Randolph Hearst. Though commercially unsuccessful, it showed how critical biographical work *should* be conducted in a genuine democracy. Regularly voted the greatest film ever made, it is "infinitely re-viewable, re-debatable," in the words of critic Laura Mulvey. *Book cover reproduced by kind permission of the British Film Institute.*

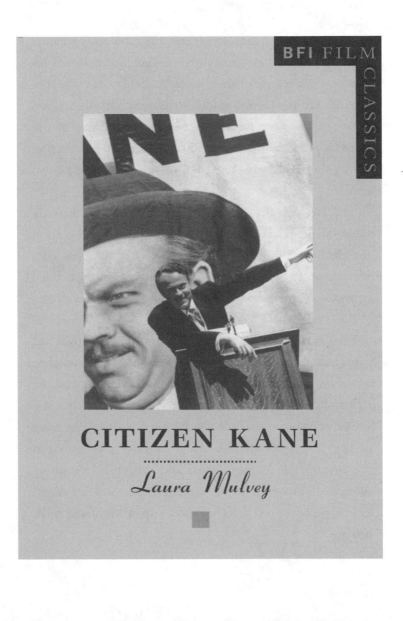

BFI FILM
CLASSICS

CITIZEN KANE

Laura Mulvey

those of William Randolph Hearst, the fabulously wealthy purveyor of "yellow journalism"—who promptly did his best to block release of the movie. A libel lawsuit was considered. The production studio, RKO, was offered a million dollars to pulp the negatives. The author of one of the print biographies of Hearst which Welles had used in preparing the script was persuaded to sue Welles for plagiarism.

The fact was that, for all Welles's genius, the new dimension he had contributed to biography proved a commercial flop. Although in later years *Citizen Kane* was consistently voted Best Film of the Twentieth Century, it failed to recoup its investment in 1941, and more or less ruined Welles's once-meteoric career.

Seen in historical context, this extraordinary movie had simply come too soon for Western democracies, entrenched as they were in rules of life depiction that protected the rich and powerful. Yet its commercial failure, and the failure of print biographies of the time to challenge the rules of libel and decorum, did "pure" biography no good. In the 1930s, while England slept and the global economy worsened, Hitler was rearming. While America slept, Hirohito's Japan was growing more expansionist and menacing.

Biography, in the West, had proven a broken reed. Once the Japanese launched their air strike on Pearl Harbor on December 7, 1941, the fate of democracy lay no longer in critical, incisive biography but in the response of ordinary and extraordinary soldiers, sailors, and airmen.

CHAPTER 7

The People's War

Once again, a world war was to change the parameters of Western biography and autobiography. The grotesque waste of human life in the First World War had spurred Lytton Strachey into mockery of public figures in its final year, and Robert Graves into an unforgettable account of his own life in the trenches—and its gruesome *reality*—a decade after the "war to end all wars" was over. But could the democratic world wait that long, in the face of new forms of blitzkrieg and bombing, with wholesale extermination of civilians as well as combatants?

Fortunately, ordinary individuals outside Germany were for the most part unimpressed by Hitler's racist ideology,

let alone his methods. Popular biographical characterization, in a familiar British marching song, of the unmarried
Führer as a man with but a single ball, and of Hitler's dep-
uty, Reichsmarschall Goering, as a batoned aviator with
two ("but they are very small"), might have been difficult
to substantiate in an English libel suit, but they epitomized a simple, working-class refusal to go along with
systematic butchery. With the advent of World War II,
moreover, journalists and broadcasters reported for the
first time from the battlefront—bringing the gritty, deathly
reality of modern hostilities to the public's attention in
what became truly a *people's* war.

It is impossible to overstate the impact of such a
world conflict on Western society. For the most part, kings
and queens had departed after World War I; now, with
World War II, the *peoples* of the threatened democracies
had been compelled and conscripted, down to air raid war-
dens, to fight for the freedoms and values they wished to
preserve—and ultimately, after many defeats, evacuations,
surrenders, and reverses, they triumphed. With the fall of
Berlin in 1945, Hitler's suicide, the dropping of the atomic
bomb, and the surrender of Japan, democracy prevailed:
the triumph not of one man's will (as Riefenstahl would
have it), but of millions of *individuals'* wills.

In Britain, no grand estates or monetary awards were

17. World War II changed the face, literally, of Western biography. Here, Shirley Slade, a trainee ferry pilot for the U.S. Air Force, is photographed by Peter Stackpole at Avenger Field, Texas, in 1943. She was one of many "ordinary" individuals featured on the front cover of *Life* magazine and in its pages during the war. *Copyright © Time-Life Pictures / Getty Images.*

given to the generals—who had to make money for their retirement by writing their autobiographies, in competition with ordinary soldiers.

The writing, in terms of biographical audience and *subjects* for biographizing, was on the wall. This time, moreover, the warning was cast in an array of biographical media, and in a plethora of biographical forms, from cinematic projection to theatrical dialogue, from radio documentary to dramatized reenactment. Moreover, very soon the business of "biography," the collective name for biographical inquiry in all media, would inhabit a tiny screen that would fit in every democratic living room: television.

The "New Biography"—by people, on behalf of the people, and about individual people, produced across a broad spectrum of popular new media—was in this sense a wholly modern phenomenon.

In the surviving dictatorships throughout the world, from Leningrad to Madrid, Haiti to Peking, "biography" might still exist as state-censored propaganda with a heavy stamp, but in the democracies the pursuit of biography now began to flourish as never before. Thanks to World War II, biography had finally found a new sociopolitical *significance* in an open society. People were sick of ideology—and, as Disraeli had remarked almost a hundred years before, biography was, mercifully, "history without theory."[1]

Postwar Biography

What had happened to change the course of biography's long history? After difficult years of appeasement, defeat, and retreat, the Western democracies had found their courage and soul, expressed in *individuals*.

This point cannot be overstressed. Though the war had taken place on many fronts, in many theaters and many countries, upon land and sea, in the air and in the depths of the oceans, involving vast armies, navies, and air forces, it had also affected *civilians* in a wholly new way, in both the industrial and the agricultural sectors of the war effort, and as victims of aerial bombing. After years of appeasement, *individuals* had become determined to fight, and if necessary to die, for the freedom to *be* individuals.

As a result, the world in which print biographers had traditionally produced their largely unchallenging, unimaginative, inartistic, psychologically deficient, and sexually prim work was truly history. It was over. Not only was Winston Churchill voted out of office in the war's aftermath, but now that President Roosevelt had died it was no longer so incumbent upon a democratic public, or its biographical functionaries, to extol *respectability*. With wartime paper controls lifted, newspapers increased in size. Print biography exploded—as did broadcast biography, televised programming about real lives, and biographical film.

The sheer volume of war memoirs, autobiographical accounts, and portraits outran statistical analysis. "I have often thought that there has rarely passed a life of which a judicious and faithful narrative would not be useful," Samuel Johnson had once remarked in an essay on biography.[2] The time for that had come at last. *Individuality* had won out in World War II: it was now rampant, celebrated, and—in growing confrontation with ideological Communism in a fast-freezing Cold War—it became clear from the outpourings of women, blacks, homosexuals, postcolonials, and other hitherto marginalized minorities that biographical depiction and self-depiction would never again be permitted, by audiences or practitioners, to kowtow to respectability.

Tabula Rasa

Biography, as the representation of real, individual human lives, now openly embraced the uninhibited individual *self*—a populist love affair that defined and still defines the biographical quest today.

Perhaps Albert Camus' 1942 account of a fictional life, *L'Etranger*—translated in Britain as *The Outsider* and in the

———∞∞∞———

General George S. Patton's aide-de-camp, *Charley Codman, records his arrival at the notorious Nazi concentration camp Buchenwald, on April 15, 1945:*

Inside the gate is a spacious yard of rough flagstones. By prearrangement, our Military Government officer and a number of French prisoners were waiting for us. . . .

The unusual feature is the basement. Here, according to eye-witnesses whom I have no reason to disbelieve, were brought prisoners condemned of capital crimes—for example, attempting to escape, insubordination, stealing a potato, smiling in ranks—usually in groups of twenty or so at a time. They were lined up against the walls, each one under a hook fixed at a height of about eight feet from the floor. (The hooks are no longer there. They were hastily removed the day we came in, but the emplacements are clearly visible.) A short slip-noose was placed about the neck of the condemned, who was then raised by the guards the distance necessary to affix the end of the noose to the hook.

If the ensuing strangulation took too long a time to suit the mood of the guards, they beat out the brains of the condemned with a long-handled club resembling a potato masher. (Specimens of the nooses and "potato mashers" are on view in the basement.) The remains were then placed on an elevator which lifted them directly to the crematory proper, the final run being made on a miniature railway of metal litters leading from the elevator platform to the furnace doors. Efficient.

Charles Codman, *Drive: A Chronicle of Patton's Army* (Boston: Little, Brown, 1957), pp. 285–286.

United States as *The Stranger*—best illustrated the new refusal to collude with the expectations of authority figures
in figuring out how to live one's life, and how to *think*
about life. As Camus wrote in an Afterword in 1955, his
outsider hero, Meursault, "refuses to lie. Lying isn't only
saying what isn't true. . . . He says what he is, he refuses
to hide his feelings and society immediately feels threatened."[3] Portrayed with pitiless honesty as an existential,
wholly ordinary, and unambitious character in a world
without credible God, Camus' unromantic antihero won
the author celebrity, the Nobel Prize, a collection of beautiful mistresses, and an early death while driving to meet
three of the latter in Paris in 1960.[4]

By now it was not only the barriers of social respectability that were being lifted in the arts. The whole field of
biographical depiction was a tabula rasa, as the antiheroes
of the day demanded not only to change the approach and
media of biography, but also *to be heard by it:* blacks, Jews,
feminists, Beats, homosexuals, hippies, druggies, trans-
sexuals . . . Confessional populist autobiography simply
kicked down the doors of biographical depiction, demanding more intimate, more challenging, more *revealing* exposure of the individual self and selves—exposure that would
also permit the burgeoning population of citydwellers to

cast off the restrictions of rural morality and recognize, in the accounts of others' lives, their own.

Anti-Communism played a major role in this development, for although it had its quasi-fascist side-effects (such as McCarthyism and the domino-theorized war in Vietnam), the postwar democratic struggle demanded critical new approaches to both self-depiction and the depiction of others. In the interests of democracy, biographers had been licensed, literally, by the Western powers at the end of World War II to subvert the idealization of "great men" like Hitler. An example had been the authorization of a young intelligence officer in the British Army, a former Oxford don who had been commissioned to counter Soviet claims that Hitler had been saved and spirited away into a secret hiding place by the wicked, capitalist Allies. Hugh Trevor-Roper's book *The Last Days of Hitler* (1947) portrayed the dead Führer as a sick, mentally deranged maniac, surrounded by a cast of operatic figures (Goering, Goebbels, and others) worthy only of ridicule. In its *anti-propagandist* way, it seemed inadvertently to set the stage for a postwar democratic play on reputations, the better to empower "ordinary" readers as citizens of a free and democratic world.

In effect, a new, democratic, postwar Western *counter-*

Novelist James Baldwin, in his postwar autobiography, recalls what it was like to work in defense plants in New Jersey in 1942 for America's war effort, yet to be refused service in a restaurant because of his color:

She did not ask me what I wanted, but repeated, as though she had learned it somewhere, "We don't serve Negroes here." She did not say it with the blunt, derisive hostility to which I had grown so accustomed, but, rather, with a note of apology in her voice, and fear. This made me colder and more murderous than ever. I felt I had to do something with my hands. I wanted her to come close enough for me to get her neck between my hands.

So I pretended not to have understood her, hoping to draw her closer. And she did step a very short step closer, with her pencil poised incongruously over her pad, and repeated the formula: ". . . don't serve Negroes here."

Somehow, with the repetition of that phrase, which was already ringing in my head like a thousand bells of a nightmare, I realized that she would never come any closer and that I would have to strike from a distance. There was nothing on the table but an ordinary mug half full of water, and I picked this up and hurled it with all my strength at her. She ducked and it missed her and shattered against the mirror behind the bar. And with that sound, my frozen blood abruptly thawed, I returned from wherever I had been, I *saw*, for the first time, the restaurant, the people, with their mouths open, already, as it seemed to me, rising as one man, and I realized what I had done, and where I was, and I was frightened. I rose and began running for the door.

James Baldwin, *Notes of a Native Son* (New York: Beacon Press, 1990; orig. pub. 1955), pp. 96–97.

opera was thus beginning, imbued with a color, vivacity, and diversity that would have made even the bourgeois Führer squirm in his grave. (The Soviet authorities had found and deliberately concealed his burned remains.) *All* reputations were now liable to be examined by revisionist historians and biographers in the West—without exception. Winston Churchill, the man who more than any other had guided the fortunes of democracy in defeating Hitler, was a prime example. He had, in Macaulay-like cadences, gilded his own wartime lily in his World War II memoirs (making it possible, wits remarked, for him to win the war not once but twice). The moment Sir Winston passed away in 1965, however, he lost the draconian protection of British libel law. Lord Moran, his physician, had watched him at close quarters throughout the war—and with the patient's demise was finally empowered to ignore the *quid pro apologia* of his peerage and publish the account that he'd drawn up, in his diaries, of the prime minister's strange personality—which encompassed not just strategic genius but depression, drink, and reliance on second-rate cronies.

In short, the biographer of the Western world, unlike J. M. Synge's Playboy, was now becoming *legitimately* subversive—speaking to an avid audience, and with progressively fewer legal restrictions.

The Magic Bullet

What barricades remained to be stormed in biography, by the 1960s? Let us pause here to review the history of biography's hurdles.

Despite its reputation as a commemorative art, biography had always been a potentially dangerous pursuit. Even as encomium, one man's reverential task was another's blasphemy or sedition—as early "alternative" Christians, and followers of Oliver Cromwell after his death, had learned. "What they have published . . . is totally unlike what has been handed down to us from the apostles," Irenaeus, the bishop of Lyons, complained about the Gnostics' version of the life of Jesus of Nazareth around 180 A.D.[5] He condemned them, Intifada-style, as heretics; and Cromwell's extollers were lucky if they avoided the same ax as Charles I's executioners.

It had been the response (seizure, interrogation, book burning, people burning) of the Christian Church to heresy or blasphemy that had molded censorship law in Britain. The Catholic monarch of England, Queen Mary, for example, *specifically* incorporated the Stationers' Company so that it might regulate the English printing trade—and thus help Romish clergy to stamp out the Protestant Reformation. Her Anglican successor then used the same Stationers' Company to do the same in reverse: to support the English church, rather than the Romish church.

In turn, the Stationers' Company, representing the printing and publishing trade in England, became the instrument of the Stuarts *against* the Puritans, in the early seventeenth century. After that, it became the instrument of the Puritans against *their* royalist enemies, when the Puritans came to power—leading Parliament to pass what was entitled *An Act for Preventing the Frequent Abuses in Printing Seditious Treasonable and Unlicensed Bookes and Pamphlets and for Regulating of Printing and Printing Presses* (1662). After the Restoration, the Censorship Act was used as an instrument of the royalists *against* the Puritans. For a brief time, it then became the instrument of the triumphant Whigs, after the "Glorious Revolution" of 1688.

Such acts of political and religious censorship were, moreover, backed by laws of *libel*—prohibitions in English civil society against the criminal defamation of powerful persons. Those in power—and those wielding power, including monarchs, nobles, judges, and their representatives—thus formed a new, often unseen Inquisition, requiring that permission be obtained prior to any printing or theatrical presentation—especially those involving living or recently deceased people.

Such tactics, in the rise of democracy, did not go uncontested. Anticensorship protests were voiced early in the seventeenth century, as printing begat popular literacy, and literacy begat questioning. The work that had the most lasting influence on the anticensorship movement was undoubtedly John Milton's *Areopagitica: A Speech for the Liberty of Unlicensed Printing to the Parliament of England* (1644), arguing against what would become known as "prior restraint." (This was an appeal for publishing rights that Milton, ironically, did not favor being extended to Catholics.) English pleas for freedom of the press thereafter proliferated in the early part of the eighteenth century—the most celebrated being John Trenchard and Thomas Gordon's pseudonymous *Cato's Letters,* which went beyond Milton in arguing against prosecutions for seditious and criminal libel. These and similar writings had even greater influence in the colonies than at home—leading to the trial of John Peter Zenger, the publisher of the *New York Weekly Journal,* in 1735, for publishing harsh criticisms of William Cosby, King George II's governor of the province of New York.

The jury's acquittal of Zenger marked a key moment in the history of the freedom of speech in America. Indeed, as its First Amendment to the Bill of Rights, the framers of the U.S. Constitution established the right of free speech as crucial to a genuinely free democracy (though this did not stop Alexander Hamilton from being killed in a duel brought on by a defamed opponent).

Censorship for seditious defamation of character thus remained the most significant hurdle to free biography for hundreds of years, until the cultural confrontation of the 1960s took place. In Britain the 1843 Theatres Act still empowered the Lord Chamberlain to review plays, prior to performance, and exercise his rights of prohibition, wherever "he shall be of opinion that it is fitting for the preservation of good manners, decorum or of the public peace so to do to forbid the acting of any play." Libel law was in some ways even more egregious, since the financial penalties were extortionate, and there was no certain way of knowing in advance what would be considered libelous. Only death—the end of life's "fitful fever," in Shakespeare's phrase—relieved biographers in the English-speaking world of the threat of libel. But on March 9, 1964, in the United States, that protection for the rich and the famous finally came to an end—at least for prominent people—thus changing the face of biography forever.

Opening the Floodgates

L. B. Sullivan, a racist government official in the South, had in 1962 won half a million dollars in punitive fines in

Alabama against the *New York Times,* which had published an advertisement that defamed him as a violent opponent of civil rights—indeed, by 1964 libel suits worth more than $300 million were pending against newspaper organizations.

The Alabama decision was, however, unanimously reversed by the Supreme Court. The justices, hearing the evidence, found the newspaper *not* guilty of reckless disregard for the truth about Sullivan, and ruled that the importance of free debate in a democratic society was more important than factual errors that might upset or even damage public officials. To win a libel case, public officials now needed to prove that damaging statements were printed with malicious intent—the Supreme Court defining "malice" as "a reckless disregard for the truth, or advance knowledge of falsity."

Questions immediately arose as to who was, and who was not, a "public official"; and it was for this reason that the Supreme Court eventually changed the term to "public figure." From that moment, journalists and biographers became free to examine, record, and interpret the lives of prominent *living* individuals with impunity, so long as there was no reckless or malicious disregard for the truth— with the burden of proof being placed not on the biographer, but on the *public figure.*

For biography in the Western world, this was a decision that would affect every biographical and autobiographical work produced thereafter, freeing authors and broadcasters, portraitists and biographical journalists, within reason, to come into the twentieth century, and to fulfill Samuel Johnson's vision of biography as an account that included both virtue *and* vice. The former frontier posts of "biography" as the printed record of whole lives were now kicked down, as artists, writers, filmmakers, broadcasters, researchers, and others sought in every medium to discover and interpret more about the lives of individuals, for a variety of motives that ranged from the political to the personal.

One by one, censorship laws in Britain and America were challenged—and fell. The sexually explicit works of writers such as James Joyce, D. H. Lawrence, Henry Miller, Lawrence Durrell, and Anaïs Nin could at last be published, while the Lord Chamberlain's stranglehold on the English stage was abolished in 1968.

The effect on biographical output was nothing less than phenomenal. Once fossilized as a Victorian journeyman's craft, the pursuit of biography now began to encompass informational, critical, and creative overlaps and crossovers with almost every art, every discipline, and every field of human knowledge and interest. Biography's floodgates opened—loosing a tidal wave of real-life depiction. Ian Hamilton on Robert Lowell, Hermione Lee on Willa Cather, Humphrey Carpenter on Ezra Pound, Curtis Cate on George Sand, Herbert Lottman on Camus, Doris Kearns on Lyndon Johnson, Leon Edel on Henry James, Antonia Fraser on Mary Stuart, D. Clayton James on Mac-Arthur, Margaret Forster on Elizabeth Barrett Browning, Philip Magnus on Edmund Burke, Winifred Gérin on the Brontës, Joseph Lash on Eleanor Roosevelt, Claire Tomalin on Katherine Mansfield—the sheer quality of biographical portraiture in print increased a hundredfold, while the same proved true of biographical theater, radio, television, and film. Had there existed a Museum of Biography and Biographers, the three decades from 1960 to 1990 would have made the National Portrait Galleries of London and Washington seem very thin: documented, dramatized, staged, filmed, fictionalized, and half-fictionalized portraits in every medium abounded in the most astonishing display of biographical outpouring ever witnessed. It was a veritable second Renaissance—a passionate, irrepressible fascination with individuality and individuals that could not be stopped, however much academics sniffed at the genre.

Yet suddenly, in an unexpected counterattack, French theorists attempted to snuff it out.

CHAPTER 8

Death of the Author

Biography had never taken root very deeply in France; the works of André Maurois and even imaginative practitioners such as Henri Troyat sold more books in English translation than in French. Hence, the end of biography seemed to French academics almost logical, once existentialism and structuralism gave way, in the 1960s and 1970s, to poststructuralism, deconstruction, and postmodernism.

The new movement was prompted by a group of intellectuals who disliked the notion of grand narratives in history, biography, or science. Most of all, they resented the *authors* of such narratives. Critics, not authors, were the truly creative force in the modern literary world, they maintained, since the critic controlled reception and interpretation. Roland Barthes thus famously declared the "death of the Author"—sending academic literary studies into a worldwide funk, as every assumption not only of authorship but of meaning was questioned, deconstructed, and found wanting. "Truth," as a black-and-white concept, was a particular casualty, and this loss drove historians into paroxysms of fury.

M. M. Bakhtin, a Marxist scholar of language philosophy, had already launched the investigation of literary representation and self-representation in Russia in the 1920s, formulating the notion that "word is a two-sided act," determined "equally by whose word it is and for whom it is meant. As a word, it is precisely the product of the reciprocal relationship between speaker and listener, addresser and addressee. Each and every word expresses the 'one' in relation to the 'other.' I give myself verbal shape," he added tellingly, "from another's point of view—ultimately from the point of view of the community to which I belong." This applied as much to a person's "inner world and thought," Bakhtin claimed, as to the outer world.[1]

Despite the collapsing bubble of the Soviet Union, and the vilification of Communist ways of thinking about language and about society, Bakhtin's ideas did not die; they were resurrected by a phalanx of French critics such as

Jacques Lacan, Ferdinand de Saussure, Jean-Pierre Oudart, Oswald Ducrot, Jean Laplanche, Jacques Derrida, and Roland Barthes, who in 1967 asserted that the author was no longer to be seen as the real owner of his or her work. Instead, the critical reader—or the critic *as* reader—was crowned king in French academia. The *reader,* not the writer, became the savant; the author was relegated to the role of servant. "Classic criticism," Barthes fumed, "has never paid any attention to the reader; for it, the writer is the only person in literature. We are now beginning to let ourselves be fooled no longer by the arrogant antiphrastical recriminations of good society in favour of everything it sets aside, ignores, smothers, or destroys; we know that to give writing its future, it is necessary to overthrow the myth: the birth of the reader must be at the cost of the death of the Author."[2]

Even Michel Foucault, who would investigate the historiography of sexuality with such brilliance, could write in 1969 (translated into English in 1977): "The name of an author remains at the contours of texts—separating the one from the other, defining their form, and characterizing their mode of existence. It [the name of the author] points to the existence of certain groups of discourse and refers to the status of this discourse within a society and culture."[3]

Deconstructed and ridiculed as a mythical fabrication of "discourse," human identity, encompassed in an individual author's name, was thus trashed, and with it (*pace* the new prophets of poststructuralism) biography and autobiography as anything more than incantations by imposters.

Fortunately, academe did not control either biography or autobiography, which went along pretty much in the same vein, regardless of the doomsayers. As Christopher Butler has written: "'realist' history and novel writing, film making, and newspaper reporting" simply "continued on their way in the era of postmodernist theory; they had a high level of general acceptability, so that many of those attracted to postmodernist art and theory must have found themselves living in two opposing epistemological worlds."[4]

Biographical authors, for the most part, simply ignored the Barthesian onslaught, since they had always—as Marjorie Garber later noted—accepted the instability of definitive factual "truth" where people are concerned, especially recollections or memories of events.[5] In an age where (in America at least) the legal veil masking the true character and actions of living public figures had, after centuries of purdah, been removed by Supreme Court verdict, biographers were far more interested in recording, as best they could, the real lives and personalities of their chosen subjects, however much French theorists might scoff at the practice. Not only were they finally licensed to explore the famous "secrets d'alcôve" first glimpsed in the nineteenth century by the French neurologist Jean-Martin Charcot, but they were giving voice at last to tens of thousands of individuals who had for centuries been off-limits to biographers, whether owing to patriarchy, sexism, racism, or other Victorian "values."

To the chagrin of Roland Barthes—who despised the universalist assumptions of a French culture that did not include him—the lives of authors, especially French authors (Balzac, Baudelaire, Zola, Proust, Sand, Dumas, Hugo, Rousseau, Gide, Colette), now proved popular in the English-speaking world as never before.

Destructors, Not Constructors

Roland Barthes, in the 1960s, was of course doing no more than Camus had done in the 1940s and '50s: subversively dislodging the present from the sentimentalities of the past. Such poststructuralist critics might lack Camus' genius for storytelling and characterization (insisting, by contrast, upon their moral right as critics to write unreadable prose), but their deconstructions of hitherto accepted notions, approaches, and agendas did spur biographers to take an even more skeptical stance toward hitherto accepted ideas. The "death of the Author" might not be taken seriously (especially by copyright lawyers), but the "deconstruction" process was often considered worthwhile, as audiences, spectators, and readers questioned the validity of old biographical lenses and encouraged the use of new ones—however subversive.

Ultimately, however, postmodernist theorists offered no credible alternative to the *grand récit* of life chronicling. Women were especially discouraged by the poststructuralist onslaught, since in "undermining women's sense of their own agency and sense of selfhood, [the poststructuralists] deny any reappropriation of women's own history," Butler noted. The "incompatibility of postmodern attitudes with a commitment to any settled position (which a good Derridean would then deconstruct)" had made French theory exciting to students rebelling against traditional hierarchical structures and attitudes, as in the great student riots of May 1968, but a dead end for biographers seeking any alternative to *récit*—whether *grand* or *petit*. Barthes's 1975 autobiography, *Roland Barthes by Roland Barthes,* was and remained largely ignored: an unsightly blemish in the history of biographical narrative, a history that went back thousands of years. Few were surprised when New York physicist Alan Sokal submitted a spoof article, entitled "Transgressing the Boundaries: Toward a Transformative

Hermeneutics of Quantum Gravity," to the literary periodical *Social Text*—and the journal unwittingly printed it in the Spring–Summer 1996 issue. In the essay, Sokal posited that "physical 'reality' is at bottom a social and linguistic construct," and larded the paper with postmodernist nonsense. After its publication he penned an exposé, which *Social Text* refused to publish. "My concern over the spread of subjectivist thinking," he later explained, "is both intellectual and political. Intellectually, the problem with such doctrines is that they are false (when not simply meaningless). There *is* a real world; its properties are *not* merely social constructions; facts and evidence *do* matter. What sane person would contend otherwise? And yet, much contemporary academic theorizing consists precisely of attempts to blur these obvious truths—the utter absurdity of it all being concealed through obscure and pretentious language."[6]

It became clear that the Author was alive, not dead—and that poststructuralism, for all its rhetoric, had no viable alternative to offer. "The best that one can say here," Butler concluded, "and I am saying it, is that postmodernists are good deconstructors, and terrible constructors."[7]

CHAPTER 9

New Directions

e have seen, in our survey, how the biographical imperative evolved over the centuries in
the West, and how it burst into fresh flower in the 1960s,
after two world wars. But if the Victorian notions of propriety and privacy in biography were finally overthrown,
and poststructuralists like Barthes and Derrida were exposed and derided, what—ethically, socially, historically,
psychotherapeutically—was the *role* of biography in the af-
fluent capitalist society of the late twentieth century? Was
it the age-old ritual of commemoration? Deeper insight
into personality, identity, and the self? Factual record? The
raising of individuals and groups from obscurity? Entertainment? Artistic license, especially in autobiography?

The short answer must be: all of the above—a plurality of motives and agendas that still characterize biography as it is practiced in different forms and in different media today.

In 1927, Harold Nicolson had predicted that print biography as a "branch of literature" might in time cease to exist, for people interested in "all the facts" would demand biographical work as information—thus spelling the ruin of biography as *art*. "The scientific interest, as it develops, will become insatiable," Nicolson lamented as a stylist; "no synthetic power, no genius for representation, will be able to keep the pace. Scientific biography will become specialized and technical. . . . There will be medical biographies—studies of the influence on character of the endocrine glands, studies of internal secretions," he prophesied, without enthusiasm.[1]

Regretting the demise of "pure" biography, Nicolson had nevertheless hoped against hope that literary writers would "discover a new scope, an unexplored method of conveying human experience."[2] And in the late twentieth-century boom in biographical output in every medium, with a constantly expanding repertoire of forms, Nicolson's hopes—at least with regard to the range of biography—were fulfilled. Authors and filmmakers who had never been drawn to the depiction of real lives now felt free to portray genuine lives and to explore them through fictional, filmic, and other narrative techniques. The short-story writer Truman Capote, for example, published one of the most electrifying of such records: *In Cold Blood* (1966), a true murder story with its intercut, cinematically vivid, gruesome portrayal of a modern, real-life nuclear family and their two dysfunctional assassins.

Capote thought that his contribution to literature was the "nonfiction novel," but he might more accurately have termed it "fiction-style biography." Certainly, Capote's work demonstrated the intimate new connection between manuscript and script—*In Cold Blood* becoming, the year after its publication, a Hollywood movie. Biopics, whether of individual lives or groups of real lives, became the rage—popular not only in Hollywood but in para-Hollywood, as the television studios began to buy the film and broadcasting rights to biographical and autobiographical narratives as fast as they bought the rights to fictional ones.

Flaubert's Parrot

In the wake of the Sixties, other traditional boundaries gave way in the field of life depiction. Biographical work was no longer limited to conventional lifespans. Authors, playwrights, and filmmakers now claimed the right to address *fragments* of lives, too. Following the Russian novelist

Aleksandr Solzhenitsyn's Nobel Prize–winning novella *One Day in the Life of Ivan Denisovitch,* even single days in the life of an individual, from President Lincoln to John F. Kennedy, were chronicled. Nor did biographies now end with the death of the subject. Increasingly, the *consequences* of a person's death fascinated consumers of biographies; William Manchester's *Death of a President* (1968) outraged the slain leader's young widow with its intimate revelations of her mourning, yet provided a spellbinding account of the president's earthly afterlife, rather than the life itself. Nor was biography limited to celebrities: Andy Warhol memorably proclaimed the right of *every* citizen, not just Kane, to his or her fifteen minutes of fame.

In sum, any or all of birth, childhood, early years, life, career, relationships, death, and the afterlife of a real individual (even an individual animal) were now encompassed in the pursuit of biography—a situation deftly parodied in the most brilliant of spoof-biographies since Virginia Woolf's *Orlando:* Julian Barnes's entrancing *Flaubert's Parrot* (1984), written in a mocking yet semi-serious vein which captivated the very same Paris-led deconstructors Barnes was, in part, lampooning.

In what might be called "The Case of the Stuffed Parrot of Croisset" (Croisset was Flaubert's hometown), a fictional English novelist rehearses, chapter by chapter, in a blend of fiction and fact, every conceivable biographical approach to the subject of Gustave Flaubert's life, work, and loves. Barnes thus pointed to the impossibility of a definitive version of a life; and in questioning the notion of a stable, single point of view, he drew an analogy with fishing. A fishing net, he pointed out through his narrator, can be seen either as "a meshed instrument designed to catch fish" or, alternatively, as a "collection of holes tied together with string."[3] Who *was* the real Flaubert—and could a biographer ever hope to catch all of the different fish associated with his life? Why had he never married? What was the private life of the man who had created Madame Bovary—the most famous imaginary adulteress, alongside Anna Karenina, in modern literature? And, Barnes asked, was it right to pose such questions, rather than resting content with Flaubert's texts?

It was a salient query, since Flaubert himself had done everything possible to confound future biographers and put them off his biographical scent. This had, of course, only inflamed posthumous curiosity—especially sexual curiosity, after World War II.

With each succeeding decade since the French writer's death, more letters and diaries had been discovered. In an age of newly legitimized and growing obsession with human sexuality, the question of Flaubert's homosexuality or

—⟨∞⟩—

Julian Barnes's award-winning spoof life of the French master-novelist of adultery consists of fifteen chapters, each with an alternative way of looking at Flaubert. Chapter 14 kicks off with a mock British university exam paper. Section B of the exam contains ten questions, of which the candidate must respond to two. The first is on "economics":

Flaubert and Bouilhet went to the same school; they shared the same ideas and the same whores; they had the same aesthetic principles, and similar literary ambitions; each tried the theatre as his second genre. Flaubert called Bouilhet "my left testicle." In 1854, Bouilhet stayed a night in the Mantes hotel that Gustave and Louise [Flaubert's lover, Louise Collet] used to patronize: "I slept in your bed," he reported, "and I shat in your latrines (what curious symbolism!)." The poet always had to work for a living; the novelist never had to. Consider the probable effect on their writings and reputations if their finances had been reversed.

Julian Barnes, *Flaubert's Parrot* (London: Picador, 1984), pp. 174–175.

—⟨∞⟩—

bisexuality "had to be" faced, Barnes claimed, even if a phi-
losopher-writer as august as Jean-Paul Sartre declared that
Flaubert was "never homosexual; merely passive and feminine in his psychology. . . . Flaubert never committed a single homosexual act in all his life."[4] Discovery of Flaubert's
correspondence with his friend Louis Bouilhet, however,
revealed not only a procession of actresses in his life,
Barnes noted, but the homosexual "bedding of Bouilhet"
and Flaubert's admission of "a taste for Cairo bath-house
boys." As Barnes's narrator, Geoffrey Braithwaite, con-
cludes: "At last we see the whole shape of his carnality; he
is ambi-sexual, omni-experienced."[5]

"Biography"—the piscatorial catch-all term for the depiction of real individuals' "vices and virtues"—now positively *delighted* in the multiplicity of possible versions of
a life.

The Life, Not the Achievement of a Life

In *Flaubert's Parrot,* Barnes was taking on a fellow author,
dead for a hundred years. Yet even as Western biographers
reached back in time to commemorate, excoriate, reexam-
ine, deconstruct, and reconstruct the lives of past individuals, they also took it upon themselves to depict, and even
deconstruct, *living* individuals in the United States. The
British parliament—still overlorded by Lords, who held

power of veto—had refused to modify the country's draconian libel laws, but such reactionary tactics could not
halt the tide of public curiosity, which—since the royal
family were known not to sue in court—was often chan-
neled into palace-watching. Celebrity adoration, in fact,
became a new—and, to some, troubling—aspect of modern biography, spawning myriad tabloid journals, memorabilia, and biographical artifacts. While serious, artistically
constructed, cogently articulated biographies in print, radio, television, theater, and film were transforming an artistically moribund profession at one end of its spectrum,
at the other end the fascination with sex and celebrity
seemed to spell a Gomorrah-like doom. In 1988 Lord
Keynes's official biographer—himself ennobled as Lord
Skidelsky for his work—complained that "the current cult
of biographical 'frankness'" was threatening to rob biography of its main, truth-telling purpose: the illumination of
the "extraordinary things" that extraordinary people accomplish. Indeed, Skidelsky railed, invasive biographical
candor had "become an end in itself, part of the current
obsession with the private lives of the famous, dignified by
a high-sounding programme of 'truth-telling' in much the
same way as journalists defend tittle-tattle about the Royal
Family in the name of the 'public interest.'"[6]

Written before the War of the Waleses and a world fascination with Princess Diana and her high-speed death, this was prophetic—though Lord Skidelsky, as a serious, old-fashioned print biographer, deplored the slide. As he lamented, "the life"—not the achievement—had become the achievement. In fact, he complained, "what used to be called the achievement is now only one accompaniment, possibly a minor one, of a style of living."[7]

Overly invasive or not, as the end of the twentieth century approached, biography—following its weak-livered showing in the years leading up to World War II—was finally showing controversial teeth, however unsightly, three and a half centuries after Sir Walter Raleigh had lost his.

CHAPTER 10

Biography Comes of Age

ueling the late twentieth-century boom in Western biography were new technologies, as well
as ever-proliferating electronic media. Indeed "the media"
was now the official designation of what had once been
called "the press." Print remained big, for traditional reasons—but television got bigger and bigger, especially with
the development of satellite and cable transmission.

Inevitably the new forms of mass communication influ-
enced the *business* of biography—a business that catered to
the growing audience for real-life reporting and depiction.
Responding to this, the young Turks of living (rather than
past) history began to feel empowered in a wholly new
way. Following successful publication of the Pentagon Pa-

pers in 1971, and the House Judicial Committee's investigation of President Nixon's abuse of executive power, the Watergate revelations changed the face of contemporary biography, via the technology of the tape recorder. The president, it was revealed under oath, had equipped the Oval Office with his own recording system, which he intended as a source of material for his eventual autobiography. Instead, it offered everyone the chance to eavesdrop on the world's most powerful man in his most private musings, and to monitor his abuses of power, thereby giving the Fourth Estate—the "gentleman of the press," as they had once been known—new license to serve the public by providing, each day, more intimate insight into current history and the figures who were making it.

Such a sea change in journalism became a sea change in biography and biographical interest. Once, like history, the record of the past, biography was increasingly becoming a record of the *present* in America. Commercial talk radio, in particular, encouraged a democratic citizenry to question current as well as past figures, as television did in every genre from lampoons to talk shows, documentaries, and dramatizations.

In the wake of Nixon's fall from grace, once-glorious, Oscar-winning Hollywood biopics such as David Lean's *Lawrence of Arabia* (1962) began to resemble the overgilded products of the *ancien régime*—which, in its time, had itself seemed amazingly fashionable and modern.

Such romanticized biopics—unlike Leni Riefenstahl's portrait of Hitler—had been enjoyed in the democracies as costume dramas by a skeptical public capable of enjoying the sentimentality (and pecs) of attractive cinematic figures (Peter O'Toole being a foot taller than his biographical subject, T. E. Lawrence), while keeping an open mind about the historical or even personal veracity of the depiction. Spurred by more challenging *television* versions of such lives, Hollywood began to put out more critical biopics—in fact, the old chain of creation, from written biography to screen biography, became redundant as creative filmmakers belatedly took up Orson Welles's baton, testing the boundaries of what could, and could not, be broadcast: boundaries still limited, however, by censorship.

Hollywood Avoids Danger

Censorship, at one level or another, is implicit in *all* human societies, even where not explicitly imposed—and America, though it was a proud democratic republic, was no exception to this rule. Researching and analyzing the cinematic biographies produced under the studio system that had operated in Hollywood from 1927 to 1960, George Custen later sought permission to explore the archives of the Motion Picture Producers and Distributors of America (MPPD), a body formed in 1922 both to publicize the cinema industry and to censor it before others tried to do so.

As Custen tells it in his *Bio/Pics: How Hollywood Constructed Public History,* he found that under the aegis of the MPPD, Hollywood had instituted an extraordinary system for self-policing via production codes (the most infamous being the Hays Code) that still exist in one form or another to this day. *Every one* of the 284 biopics produced by the major and independent American studios in the years 1930–1960 had to be submitted to the MPPD's censorship board. "Virtually no aspect of a film could be passed without the approval of this powerful organization."[1]

This was a truth which almost nobody outside Hollywood was aware of at the time, and which few people are aware of today. The code's effect on film biography can be illustrated by a single example: the Warner Brothers biopic of Dr. Paul Ehrlich, Nobel Prize–winning pioneer in the fields of immunology, chemotherapy, and syphilis treatment. The film, titled *Dr. Ehrlich's Magic Bullet* (a reference to Ehrlich's pre-penicillin, arsenic-based cure for syphilis), was rushed into production in 1940 for a very laudable political reason. As Hitler's racist ideology was fueling a second world war that threatened to engulf even isolationist America, it was deemed important by Hollywood to produce biographies of "good" Germans, and especially of Jewish Germans, who had done so much to further the cultural, social, and scientific achievements of the West. Dr. Ehrlich held a number of honorary doctorates from American universities. The Hays Office, however, insisted on changing the film's original title, *Test 606,* and pointed to the special provisions of its code, subsection II(7), which stated that "sex hygiene and venereal diseases are not proper subjects for theatrical motion pictures."[2] All mention of syphilis was thus *verboten* in the film—despite the fact that it dealt precisely with Ehrlich's invaluable work in eradicating syphilis via the "magic bullet."

Bullets of a less magical kind nevertheless abounded. Understandably, wartime censorship affected every medium, but Hollywood censorship of the most patronizing kind continued long after World War II was over. As late as 1957, Custen shows, the producers of a biopic of New York mayor Jimmy Walker were warned to "downplay his real-life adulterous" affairs[3]—not because of any libel concerns, since Walker had died in 1946, but because adultery, like homosexuality, bare breasts, drug use, and venereal disease, was still taboo in real-life Hollywood depictions.

In a world increasingly dominated by images rather than words, the ethical concerns of educators and parents were understandable. "However unfortunate, it appears likely that even well-educated Americans are learning most of their history from film and television," the historian John O'Connor has written.[4] And as Custen points out, this now put a powerful learning tool in the hands of a small number of people with disparate agendas, seeking to influence their society's historical and biographical output. "The studios tried to control, through various means, the attempts of others to shape their making of history," Custen notes; indeed, they "accomplished this—in part for reasons of efficiency, in part from ideological purposes—through standardization of the 'great man' narrative, through ritualized use of certain actors in certain parts, through control of publicity, and through adherence to legal standards of what things could be pictured about the famous, living and dead." Such legal pressures meant that, although historically accurate, "certain events" were "elided" from films "for fear of legal action." As a result, Hollywood prior to the Sixties completely failed to "turn biography into something of potential danger, a crusade with a broad social base." Instead, the heartland of motion pictures—like many other territories of biography throughout history—was content to produce culturally unchallenging love stories and tales of hard-won fame, often a mirror more to the studio head than the head of the subject.[5]

That situation was bound to be contested, given the removal of libel concerns and the new openness to human sexuality in biographical work in the 1960s and '70s. Yet how far could biographers go? An example of film biography that illustrates the challenging, demythologizing, critically interpretive, and richly imaginative challenge of the new era was, interestingly, a sort of comic anti-hagiography: *Monty Python's Life of Brian*.

Life of Brian

In their legendary film *Monty Python and the Holy Grail* (1974), Graham Chapman, John Cleese, Terry Gilliam, Eric Idle, Terry Jones, and Michael Palin had ridiculed Arthurian legends without ruffling many feathers. But their idea for a spoof biography of the real Jesus, as the son of a Roman soldier, was considerably bolder; indeed, from the perspective of a twenty-first century riven by religious intolerance, terrorism, and jihadism, their naïveté seems nothing short of extraordinary. In the context of biography in the late twentieth century, however, the film was oddly typical—probably even inevitable, as artists, scholars, and researchers of every description, from humorists to television show hosts, sought to interpret unknown lives, and reinterpret known ones.

Renewed interest in the textual evidence for Jesus' life

had already led, after World War II, to the discovery (in Egypt in 1945) and publication (in the West in the 1970s) of the Gnostic Gospels, which sparked serious discussion of Jesus' paternity. According to the Jewish Mishnah (collected religious writings dating from about 200 A.D.), Jesus' patronymic was "ben Pantera," or "son of Pantera"—with suggestions that Pantera had been a Roman soldier stationed in Palestine. In Bingerbrück, Germany, a tombstone came to light with the inscription "Here lies Tiberius Julius Abdes Pantera of Sidon, age sixty-two, a soldier of forty years' service [including Palestine], of the first cohort of archers."[6] But in view of Christian doctrine concerning the Virgin Birth, how could such speculations be aired without accusations of blasphemy, which had been proscribed by codified laws for centuries? The Python team soon found out.

Jesus Christ Superstar (1973), a musical biography by Tim Rice and Norman Jewison, with a score by Andrew Lloyd-Webber, had already skated on thin ice in depicting Jesus' life on stage and then on screen, but its producers had remained on the right side of blasphemy laws by accepting Jesus' divinity. The Monty Python team had an alternative agenda—and when the EMI corporation withdrew funding for their Jesus epic during filming in North Africa, it looked as if religious satire was one biographical frontier

that could still *not* be breached in the West. Only an infu-
sion of funds from the millionaire Beatle George Harrison
enabled the film to avoid being shelved by its nervous producers. Furthermore, the Pythons had to make it clear that
the movie was *not* a life of Jesus: they titled it *Life of Brian*
and filmed a new opening scene, in which Brian's birth
takes place down the road from that of Jesus, simultaneously, in another Nazareth manger. Only in this way did
the Monty Python team escape legal indictment under
current blasphemy laws, especially in America. (As it was,
the "Otto sequence," in which Jewish terrorists vowed to
"set up a Jewish state that's going to last for a thousand
years," was cut, as well as an additional forty minutes of
material, from the original two-hour film.)

Behind its wacky humor, *Life of Brian,* released in 1979,
had a passionate agenda: it urged people to resist the se-
duction of cult hysteria and fanatical groups, encourag-
ing them to maintain the skepticism and independence of
mind that is the birthright of every individual in a free society. The film culminated in a haunting plea by Brian, an ordinary man mistaken for the Messiah, to the populace of
Jerusalem: "Think for yourselves, you're all individuals!"
With this appeal, the film might well stand as a landmark
in the history of modern biography, just like *Citizen Kane.*
In farcical parody, it encapsulated the fascination and prob-

lems endemic to Western biography of the late twentieth century. In a key scene, a crowd below Brian's window responds in unison to his exhortation that each person think for himself:

CROWD: Yes, we're all individuals.

BRIAN: You're all different.

CROWD: Yes, we *are* all different.

DENNIS: I'm not.

CROWD: Sssshhh!

BRIAN: Well, that's it. You've got to work it out for yourselves.

CROWD: Yes, yes!! We've got to work it out for ourselves.

BRIAN: Exactly.

CROWD: Tell us more.

BRIAN: No, no, that's the point. Don't let anyone tell you what to do. Otherwise . . . Ow!

[MANDY drags him away by his ear.]

MANDY: That's enough.

[She propels him out of sight.][7]

The controversial *Life of Brian* became a grand success. Yet many people were concerned about the direction biography was taking in addressing reputations—

especially given the way it was fueled by intrusive sexual curiosity.

Portrait of a Marriage

Though Harold Nicolson had underestimated the power of "impure" biography as political propaganda in the 1920s and '30s, he had not mistaken the signs that print biographies were starting to adopt the techniques of modernist novels. Indeed, it was Nicolson who in 1927 predicted that, in tandem with scientific, informational biographies, life depiction might possibly "wander off into the imaginative," as biographers increasingly roamed the "open fields of fiction. The fictional form will be given to biography," he prophesied.[8] And he even foresaw that there would be "franker and fuller autobiographies than we have been accorded," as well as cases in which, by "some rare accident, a man of talent" would compose "a good inductive biography of some arresting personality with whom he has been intimate."[9]

Whether Nicolson could have imagined that his *own* life would ever be the subject of such inductive disclosure—indeed, that it would be his *own son* who would posthumously "out" him and his lesbian wife, as Freud had once outed Leonardo—must remain a matter of speculation.

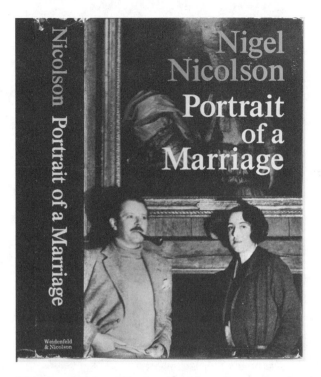

18. With the relaxation of legal and social mores, sexual candor characterized biography in the final decades of the twentieth century in all the biographical arts. Nigel Nicolson's *Portrait of a Marriage* (1973), written by the son of Harold Nicolson and Vita Sackville-West, narrated his parents' homosexual life stories with riveting honesty, and his book was eventually dramatized as a BBC television series. *First-edition jacket photo; reproduced by permission of Weidenfeld and Nicolson / Orion Publishers, London.*

———◦∞◦———

In making public his mother's private lesbian confession
fifty years after it was written, the biographer Nigel
Nicolson cautioned:

There is one essential matter which must be explained, and I prefer to do it at the outset. Vita has described her nature quite frankly: she was physically attracted by women more than by men, and remained
so all her life. She was by no means frigid, but she
came to look upon the "normal" act of love as bestial
and repulsive. . . . Once, when she was a child, a game-
keeper's son at Sluie had initiated her, by demonstration, into the physical differences between boys and
girls, and she had run away, dreadfully shocked. Her
mother's fastidiousness and her father's reluctance to

Nigel Nicolson, Sir Harold's biographer-son, had already
done a capable job of editing his father's social and political diaries in 1966 and 1968. In defending his expurgation of
those diaries, he had warned that unless biographers held
back from revealing the most intimate details of their sub-

discuss any intimate subject with her deepened her sexual isolation. . . . When I myself married, my father solemnly cautioned me that the physical side of marriage could not be expected to last more than a year or two, and once, in a broadcast, he said, "Being in love lasts but a short time—from three weeks to three years. It has little or nothing to do with the felicity of marriage." Simultaneously, therefore, and without placing any great strain upon their love for one another, they began to seek their pleasure with people of their own sex, and to Vita at least it seemed quite natural.

Nigel Nicolson, *Portrait of a Marriage* (London; Weidenfeld and Nicolson, 1973), p. 139.

jects' sexual lives, biographees might begin to "destroy their most intimate letters and be very careful with their journals."

This was an ironic injunction—for in 1973, a mere five years later, Nicolson *fils* found his mother's secret journal in a Gladstone bag, following her death, and published his bombshell *Portrait of a Marriage,* a biography of his own parents. It was not the work of a dutiful Victorian son. Reading it, elderly doyens of the literary world rubbed their eyes in disbelief. Had Nicolson *fils,* the son of a knight of the English realm, actually *dared* to expose to the world his biographer-father's homosexuality and his poet-mother's lesbianism? Was this a new form of parricide?

Nicolson had certainly dared. His mother, Vita Sackville-West, had written frankly of her passionate affair with Violet Trefusis for specific reasons, and he took those reasons as his biographical pretext. "I am not writing this for fun," Vita had noted as far back as September 27, 1920. Rather, she was writing because, as a lesbian, she was determined to "tell the entire truth" about herself and her sexuality. Though she knew that her account could not be published in her lifetime, she was sure that eventually "the psychology of people like myself will be a matter of interest, and I believe it will be recognized that many more people of my type do exist than under the present day system of hypocrisy is commonly admitted."[10]

Nicolson's portrait of his parents, published sixty-six years after Gosse's anonymous *Father and Son,* thus broke yet another taboo in biographical portraiture and brought print biography back into line with the scandalously revealing painted portraits of early modernism at the start of the century. The work was immensely popular; before long, a production company acquired the rights for television dramatization.

Yet unsurprisingly—and this has been true of all such revealing portraits—the book found no favor in the Middle East. It was not published in Arabic and was generally banned in Islamic cultures. For good or ill, fundamentalist mullahs refused to sanction candid biographies, any more than they were willing to tolerate blasphemous humor or whimsical tales of the Prophet Mohammed. (A fatwa was issued against the author of the *Satanic Verses*, Salman Rushdie, for indulging in precisely this sort of whimsy.) The upshot was that biography became not only the new symbol of democratic freedoms enjoyed in the West—especially for the way it challenged laws protecting the rich, the powerful, and the famous—but also the expression of a defining borderline separating East and West at the end of the twentieth century. In Western multicultural societies embracing new technologies such as the Internet, biographical curiosity and information drove or accompanied every advance in the 1990s, humanizing portraiture to an extent inconceivable a century before, when prominent people were depicted as matchstick men. Now reality became almost surreal: even the penis of the president of the United States could be a matter of public curiosity and living history, with the name of his accuser (Paula Jones) and that of his avid-for-explicit-details prosecutor (Ken Starr) giving further credence to Warhol's epigram on fame. Almost every internal boundary now came up for challenge. Filmmakers, broadcasters, editors, viewers, audiences, readers, and others who peopled the biographical bazaar were ravenous for celebrity stories, as well as obscure biographies: simple narratives, complex narratives, interpretations, spoof narratives, and antinarratives; full lives, half lives, fragments of lives, days in the life of, life after the death of . . .

Television, especially, gloried in the biographical—spawning countless programs about notorious figures on the one hand, and Everyman or Everywoman on the other. It was as if Western society was undergoing a mass search for self, in which the life stories of real people were now felt to be more vital, more authentic, more accessible, and more revealing than the fictional lives that artists and writers had produced for several thousand years as models of good behavior, and warnings of bad behavior. The quest for such real lives became all-embracing and all-intrusive, stealing back from traditional novelists the very meat and much of the purpose of their art.

The result was that biographers were not simply permitted legally, but were also impelled by public curiosity and demand, to peer into the private lives of real people—leaving fiction writers and broadcasters either to seek out relatively unexplored corners of life (such as the paranormal) or to adapt by *co-opting* biographical facts and experiences for fictionalized versions of real lives. Thomas Keneally's novel *Schindler's Ark* (1982) was a prime example: the "true" story of Oskar Schindler presented to the judges of the Booker Prize as fiction—and winning.

Coming of Age

By the 1990s, then, every aspect of real life—every corner, every color, every gender, every status, and almost every eccentric—was liable to be exposed beneath the biographer's microscope, subjected to relentless interest and curiosity, for every conceivable motive, ranging from social work with the elderly (who were encouraged to combat depression by "editing" their own life stories as lifelines of good and bad) to psychotherapy; from the history of science to medical case histories—researchers using such material to test their understanding of the brain, consciousness, personality, and emotion, exactly as Harold Nicolson had predicted.[11] Belatedly, after decades of Marxist and post-Marxist theorizing in the social sciences, even skeptics began to recognize that their own academic bias against individual life history was the problem, not the life histories: that their generalizations were, in fact, faulty and even fatuous at the level of the individual. As William Runyan warned in 1984 (an appropriate date, given Orwell's vision of a world ruled by Thought Police), "Learning what is true about persons-in-general often has substantial limitations in enabling us to understand and predict the behavior of individuals."[12]

Harold Nicolson had also predicted that fiction—or at least the techniques and imaginative play of fiction—might be incorporated with biography, and he now proved to be right. Structurally, stylistically, ethically, and entertainingly, novelists and filmmakers had for years reveled in their license to fantasize and expose, to ridicule, traduce, and otherwise explore the dramas and tackinesses of modern culture—paraphrasing, plagiarizing, borrowing from, plundering, sexing up, dumbing down, and creatively distorting conventional images and attitudes with unceasing energy and inventiveness as they exploited the abiding power of artistic narrative, especially catharsis, to entertain as well as enlighten. Now, finally, biographers were licensing themselves to do the same—via real subjects. Impelled by the public's curiosity, which was at once voyeuristic and hungry for information—as well as by popular love of personal narratives and by academics' growing distaste for ideology and French theorizing—biography was finally coming of age.

CHAPTER 11

Biography on Trial

$\mathcal{A}$ s so often in the history of art and culture, not everyone was aware of what was happening to biography, or pleased about the direction it seemed to be taking in the final decades of the twentieth century. Many individuals in positions of power upheld attitudes of decorum and rigid rules of genre: rules that preserved libel law in Britain, for example, and stringent copyright law in America—the latter resulting in the famous trial of British poet and biographer Ian Hamilton, who in 1986 attempted to publish a new print biography of the poet and novelist J. D. Salinger.

Hamilton had found some of Salinger's early letters in American archives, and wanted to quote small extracts to demonstrate how the novelist had matured as a writer. Salinger sued to block publication of the book, claiming that Hamilton's quotation of the unpublished letters violated copyright laws and questioning standards of "fair use." Judge Pierre Leval, who presided over the suit in Manhattan, ruled that Hamilton's quotations were "too minimal to subject Salinger to any serious harm"; but Leval evidently did not understand the embittered, somewhat weird, and reclusive personality of the celebrated author of *Catcher in the Rye*. The appeals courts overruled Leval's decision, apparently of the opinion that Salinger was entitled to his privacy, which he claimed would be invaded— even though the case concerned copyright and fair-use issues, not privacy. Censoring Hamilton, the federal judges declared, would not "interfere in any significant way with the process of enhancing public knowledge of history or contemporary events."[1]

Clearly, the appeals court judges had never read any biographies, nor were they concerned that copyright law was being distorted into what could be construed as privacy-protection or quasi-libel law. Certainly they failed to recognize the evidentiary value of letters as *crucial* to the transmission of personality in life depiction; indeed, they appeared to have little notion of the difference between a biography and a history. Their ruling stuck, however, and was given the imprimatur of the U.S. Supreme Court in 1987.

Publishers of biography in America went into shock, which persists to this day. Henceforth, they would need armies of lawyers to protect them from the privacy-protectors. Meanwhile, traumatized, Hamilton had to make do with a sadly bowdlerized version of his biography. Smarting from his defeat, he then published, in 1992, his quickly classic *Keepers of the Flame: Literary Estates and the Rise of Biography,* in which he recounted the long history of copyright misuse by heirs to defend the reputations of their deceased spouses and forebears from the predations of life chroniclers—such as himself.

Hamilton's example and warnings went unheeded. In 1995 the European Union extended the period of copyright over any work—however innocuous or commercially valueless—to the author's lifetime, plus seventy years. Given the increasing lifespans in the West, this amounted in most cases to virtual perpetuity—during which no biographer could quote more than a few lines of a published document, and even less from an unpublished letter, memo, or conversation without the express permission of the subject's legal inheritors.

In the United States, where public figures had lost the right of libel protection, the EU law was seen as giving heirs enormous new compensatory powers to maintain and protect posthumous reputations—yet, to the dismay of biographers, Congress then passed the Sonny Bono Copyright Term Extension Act (1998) to keep the United States in parallel with the European Union directive. The Supreme Court struck down a challenge to the act, prompting Justice Stephen Breyer to issue a dissenting opinion on the verdict: "Its primary legal effect is to grant the extended term not to authors, but to their heirs, estates, or corporate successors. And most importantly, its practical effect is not to promote, but to inhibit, the progress of 'Science'—by which the Framers [of the Constitution] meant learning or knowledge."[2]

Once again, biography had found itself in the line of fire in the defense of democratic rights.

Reactionaries' Reaction

Judge Breyer's dissent proved small consolation for biographers denied access to their most important materials: evidence. Yet for people on the sidelines watching the fortunes of biography as life depiction in the modern world, the situation was cruelly fascinating. Restrictions on defamation and on fair use of historical materials notwithstanding, biographers in the late twentieth century were—and *felt themselves to be*—the brave new portraitists of the

Western world. They would *not* be held back. As documentarists, they had relied since Greek and Roman times on the right to quote their subjects—whether Pericles' oration or Cicero's speeches. To stop them, copyright holders had now asserted a legal right to extend their control of documentary materials into near-perpetuity, but international disagreements over copyright extension made the situation ridiculous. Canada held fast to a copyright protection term of lifetime-plus-fifty-years, while Australia declined to make its copyright law retroactive. Thus, the heirs of D. H. Lawrence (who died in 1930) and James Joyce (who died in 1941) exulted in the demise of French poststructuralist critics who had declared the death of the Author, but found themselves powerless to reestablish copyright control north of the United States, or south of Indonesia.

This did not prevent them from tilting at biographers' windmills, however. Brenda Maddox was forced to omit large chunks of material from her print biography *Nora: The Real Life of Molly Bloom* at the behest of Joyce's quixotic grandson Stephen. And in perhaps the most egregious case of copyright-law manipulation, in 2004 Stephen Joyce claimed that a biographical-literary exhibition, *James Joyce and Ulysses,* to be sponsored by the National Library of Ireland, would breach his copyright control on behalf of a grandfather already deceased for almost sixty-five years. Meanwhile, the Irish festival "ReJoyce Dublin 2004" had to do entirely without public readings from the works of James Joyce! One professor of English, throwing up his hands in despair, warned his students to avoid researching Joyce at all.[3]

As arch-victims of censorship themselves, D. H. Lawrence and James Joyce would have fumed at such censorship on the part of their heirs. But in terms of the pursuit of biography as a vibrant, challenging, modern expression of man's fascination with individuality, the battlefield that biography had become now testified to its crusading status in the arts and sciences, as reactionaries fought to keep the genre within strict rules in the run-up to the millennium, and biographers sought to subvert them.

An example was Edmund Morris, the distinguished biographer of Theodore Roosevelt. In writing the first volume of his monumental, conventional life of President Roosevelt, published in 1980, Morris had enjoyed using quasi-fictional techniques, such as imagining Teddy Roosevelt's state of mind at certain moments ("His mind was on politics, and on this evening's Republican County Convention in the Grand Opera House he was curious to see who would be nominated for Mayor of New York"). So much so, in fact, that biography watchers wondered if, in tack-

In his authorized biography of President Ronald Reagan, Edmund Morris—inventing a persona for himself as the son of a Yale-educated Jewish Episcopalian convert and Chicago cattle feeder—recalls his first recollections of "Dutch" Reagan at Eureka College in 1928:

I saw little of Dutch in class; he was majoring in sociology and minoring in economics, while I took mathematics and music. But since only freshmen ranged "'neath the elms" (a coy Eurekism one quickly tired of), Paul and I were constantly bumping into him—which is to say, bypassing him: his unique, fluid walk enabled him to negotiate strange shoals as easily as an eel. It was impossible not to see him coming, with his floppy center part and jazz-style clothes, modeled on the *Chicago Tribune*'s comic strip "Harold Teen." I recall in particular a pale-tan sport coat worn over a loud turtleneck sweater.

Manifestly lonely, Dutch was never alone. There was something attractive about the simplicity of his enthusiasms—Eddie Cantor, the Olympics, last night's social, next week's game—and his urgent desire to tell us what he already knew. Although his manner was egalitarian and friendly, the only opinions he seemed to value were those of authority figures: senior faculty, varsity players, and society officers. He was already, irremediably, a frat man, Mugs having gotten her sister's boyfriend to pledge him to Tau Kappa Epsilon. Even in those dim distant days, people did things for Dutch.

Edmund Morris, *Dutch: A Memoir of Ronald Reagan* (New York: Random House, 1999), pp. 67–68.

ling Ronald Reagan's life after being appointed Reagan's official biographer, Morris would go so far as to watch himself "watching" the president.[4] To the consternation of his literary audience, Morris—taking his cue from contemporary fiction and film—did exactly that: in the book, he watches himself, as a *participating* character in Reagan's life story, observing the events as they happened.[5]

Published in 1999, *Dutch: A Memoir of Ronald Reagan* was extremely ill-received; Morris seemed to bring down the wrath of the entire book-reading establishment. Fin-de-siècle readers of biography, it transpired, were unwilling to countenance such a radical extension of the postmodern biographer's more playful relationship with his audience (sometimes known as the *pacte,* the term that the French literary theorist Philippe Lejeune has applied to the unwritten contract between an autobiographical text and its readers).[6] Some mild speculation here, some imaginative projections there. But *inventing* one's own participation in a true-life story?

A writer of rare artistic sensibility, Morris was understandably hurt by his failure to convince the public that his 874-page tome was a work of biographical pioneering. It was left to his wife, Sylvia Jukes Morris (a distinguished biographer in her own right), to quietly remind him: "You *were* the *official* biographer, darling!"[7]

CHAPTER 12

The Miner's Canary

$\mathcal{A}$ mid discussions of the myriad forms of biographical output in the latter part of the twentieth century, a major aspect of modern biographical history that has gone virtually unexplored is the way in which biography was forced to adapt—or be adapted. After World War II, biography began to travel—to migrate across genres in a way that had not happened since early Christian times, when the life of Jesus and his disciples was interpreted and reinterpreted in every medium known to man, from Greek and Latin text to stained-glass windows.

The work of Michael Holroyd is a prime example of biography's postwar journey from print to less frequent print, and ultimately to the moving—in both senses of the word—image. As the first full-scale print biographer of Lytton Strachey, the young Holroyd built upon the work of U.S. interwar academics by attempting a methodical, *grand récit* scholarly approach that would open up the field of life depiction to the topic of homosexuality, in a period of continuing homophobia. His two-volume *Lytton Strachey: A Critical Biography* was, as one reviewer said, "the first post-Wolfenden biography" (a reference to Lord Wolfenden's overthrow in 1967 of the notorious British law that made homosexuality a crime). *Lytton Strachey* was also a magnificent example of a biographer's attempt to open a window not only onto his subject's personality, but onto an entire little-known world: the colorful subculture of the artistic and intellectual community known as "Bloomsbury."

That demi-bohemian milieu of London-based authors, painters, critics, economists, and others who had met and intermingled in the neighborhood around the British Museum fascinated Holroyd as an aspiring biographer, for the Bloomsbury era—which flourished from the 1910s to the 1930s—had, by the 1950s, gone out of fashion and largely out of mind. Carefully collecting and assembling evidence from letters, diaries, and personal interviews in order to reconstruct that lost intellectual and artistic world, Holroyd began to paint his literary group portrait around the very individual who had put an end to Victorian biography.

Holroyd's pioneering, painstaking, masterly extension of scholarly but readable print biography into a more modern genre capable of tackling the sexuality of his subjects—the homosexual Lytton Strachey and his contemporaries—not only fulfilled Sigmund Freud's original vision of free discussion of human sexuality in a biography, but inspired a new generation of print biographies in which patient scholarship demolished long-standing barriers of reticence and prudery.

That Holroyd felt impelled to press beyond these barriers reflected, of course, larger cultural changes taking place in the West in the 1960s, from the waning of sexual censorship to the rise of gay rights and feminism. His courage was deeply appreciated by (among others) the homosexual British actor Kenneth Williams, who expressed the sympathy of many when he reflected on the human being who emerged in Holroyd's portrait: "this strange, gentle, unhappy and wonderfully civilized man who was so unable to find complete & shared love, and who was, at the end, surrounded by love."[1]

Biography's power to touch the emotions as well as the intellect was a feature of the new openness. Some readers, however, were not moved—at least in the positive sense. "My mail became filled with apoplectic accusations," Holroyd later recalled.[2] Bloomsbury novelist William Gerhardie, one of the people Holroyd interviewed, called him "a *smilingly* impenitent, pig-headed, bloody-minded, bigoted, intolerant, unyielding, inelastic, *hard*, inflexible, opinionate, fanatical, obsessed, pedantic, rock-ribbed, *unmoved*, persistent, incurable, irrepressible, intractable, impersuadable, cross-grained ruffian."[3] "Even the bedrooms and beds are explored for data," another Bloomsbury survivor complained.[4] Fortunately for Holroyd, such diatribes were outweighed by effusions of praise, not only from homosexuals identifying with Strachey as their outed hero, but from fellow biographers who were pleased to see the dismantling of a sort of literary Berlin Wall.

Having initiated this challenging new approach to modern print biography (scholarly judiciousness combined with intensely moving sexual revelation), Holroyd used his hard-won knowledge of early twentieth-century subcultures to depict other lives of the period in the same way. *Augustus John* appeared in 1976, and *George Bernard Shaw* in 1988—in five volumes, subtitled *Search for Love, 1856–1898; Pursuit of Power, 1898–1918; Lure of Fantasy, 1918–1950; Last Laugh, 1950–1992;* and *Shaw Companion.*

Beyond dedicated research in archives and collections of private papers, biographers relied on insistent oral interviews—formerly the preserve of journalists, rather than historians—to move biography into the front line of challenging historical writing.[5] Sex too, as Holroyd recognized, provided the modern biographer with a weapon—one that could be used not merely, as Freud had done, to reduce the puzzle of a human being's life and creativity to a theorem (as in explaining Leonardo da Vinci's inventiveness), or solely to understand an individual in greater complexity and depth, but also to tease a modern audience into reading *more* about the subject. Sex was, in sum, a way of enticing readers toward greater empathy and knowledge.

Yet becoming deeply engrossed in the subject's life and times had its dangers. The very nature of the extended research process, often taking many years, could turn the dedicated biographer into an egghead. The serious print biographer, after Holroyd, thus came to differ very little from those otherworldly scientists who live obsessively night and day with their research projects. Holroyd himself became so entwined by, and *in*, Strachey's life that in many ways he lost contact with his own. "Over the years I was writing my book, I do not think I was ever more than half aware of the outside world," he later confessed. "The world in which I lived was that of the Bloomsbury Group during the early part of this [twentieth] century. My work held something of the excitement of an archaeological discovery. The vast *terra incognita* represented by the Strachey papers seemed like a lost way of life that was gradually emerging into the light."[6]

As Holroyd immersed himself in further Bloomsbury-period lives and wrote ever-longer print biographies—in defiance of Strachey's injunction against "those two fat volumes"—the world outside his purview altered, and began to demand a different approach.

This was a development Holroyd later candidly admitted he hadn't foreseen—that "as the performing arts began to enjoy a renaissance, there would be proposals from Christopher Hampton, Peter Luke, John Osborne, Ken Russell, Gore Vidal and others to make films and plays, and even a musical, from the Strachey and Carrington story." All were inspired by Holroyd's deeply moving account of the *nonsexual,* unrequited love felt by the painter Dora Carrington for Lytton Strachey.[7]

In writing ever longer and more serious print biographies, Holroyd failed to adapt to this situation—for wholly honorable reasons. Privileged to have been taken into the confidence of a group of sexual "inverts" ("perverts," according to the laws obtaining at the time, prior to the Wolfenden Bill), he was aware, like Nigel Nicolson, that any "sensationalized" treatment of the life story could compromise the willingness of historical witnesses to preserve, let alone permit access to, crucial documentary evidence such as letters and diaries.

Sensationalism was, however, an inexorable tide swamping Western civilization by the 1970s and '80s, and Holroyd's fading Bloomsbury stars saw this quite clearly. It was the prospect of their lives being dramatized for the screen as a result of his print-biography (which they hoped only the cognoscenti would read) that filled his surviving Bloomsbury sources with fear. One of them queried whether he would be arrested for sodomy if the biography were to be published before the change in England's anti-homosexuality law.

Yet following the 1967 legislation, the ethical stakes involved in revealing the sexual lives of real people seemed, if anything, to increase. "I am sure that most of us would have declined to let him have such access had we known that a film dramatization of the characters was to follow," Dora Carrington's brother Noel complained to the BBC. "I feel there is a valid distinction between a biography and the televised dramatization of a life, especially one that

ended in tragedy still exceedingly painful to those concerned." Dora Carrington had shot herself a few hours after Strachey passed away.[8]

The Biography Channel

What *was* the "valid distinction" between a print biography and a televised dramatization of a life?

Interestingly, Holroyd's protesters were (just) willing to
countenance a BBC *documentary* television film, but not a
"televised dramatization," let alone a Hollywood-style feature film, or biopic—a fact that indicated, among middle-
class literati at least, a sort of hierarchy of *status* in biographical treatment, descending from scholarly, multivolume works at the top, down through radio and television documentaries, to garish dramatization on TV and
(the lowest of the low) dramatization on the big screen.

Certainly Holroyd's informants were correct in fearing
the power and, perhaps, oversimplification of dramatization—for dramatization (appealing to the broadest possible audiences, in order to fund the huge costs of production) invoked substantially different rules and expectations
from those of scholarly print biography or documentary
television. To *object* to dramatization, however, was a losing battle in the late twentieth century, when the conse-

quences of mass education and mass media were apparent everywhere. Television might be winning in terms of audience numbers, yet Hollywood fought back with its larger screen and deeper pockets, thanks to worldwide distribution and video and DVD sales. The result was that it became virtually impossible to undertake multivolume print biographies, except on certain renowned subjects (Churchill, Eisenhower, Stalin, Lincoln, Franklin D. Roosevelt, and so on). In a world of faster communication and proliferation of data, attention spans had shortened, even as higher education, paradoxically, expanded. It came as no surprise when a cable TV channel devoted to life stories—the Biography Channel—was added to the panoply of choices.

Ironically, it was Holroyd's original biographee who had predicted the need for concision. "To preserve," Strachey wrote in 1918, "a becoming brevity—a brevity which excludes everything that is redundant and nothing that is significant—that, surely, is the first duty of the biographer."[9]

The Accent on Sex

Acknowledging the public's unwillingness to tolerate multivolume scholarly print biographies, Michael Holroyd adapted his own two-volume life of Strachey into a single-volume narrative, *Lytton Strachey: A Biography*. In time, however, even this had to be cut down—not only to accommodate the public's impatience with long print biographies, but also to accord with its growing fascination with sex.

Virginia Woolf had predicted this development. "What was thought a sin is now known, by the light of facts won for us by the psychologists, to be perhaps a misfortune; perhaps a curiosity"—but not, in her secular view, the work of the devil. "The accent on sex" would lead, she prophesied, to the "destruction of a great deal of dead matter still obscuring the true features of the human face." The biographer must therefore "go ahead of the rest of us, like the miner's canary, testing the atmosphere, detecting falsity, unreality, and the presence of false conventions."[10]

Print biographers had traditionally been the slowest to accommodate this shift toward exploration, especially in the area of sex—not only because of laws relating to pornography and social rules regarding print decorum (books, unlike films, carried no age-rating for content), but because, in comparison with the newer media of film and television, print biography was still, for the most part, produced by old-fashioned writers who were proud of their gentlemanly Victorian traditions of what was polite and impolite. Increasingly, print biographers were academics, whose teaching and research grants covered the cost of book research and preparation, but whose universities, as educational establishments for training the young, frowned on licentiousness. Also, more and more biographers were women, who tended to be more inhibited in seeking or parading sexual revelations. Thus, the onus or challenge of breaking taboos fell upon the graphic media.

Holroyd had, to be sure, broken the taboo on revelations about homosexuality as an integral part of the biographical picture—but this had been permitted (by copyright holders, publisher, critics, and readers) only because his very *scholarliness* implied that he was writing, like Dr. Freud, as a sort of forensic scientist—not as a voyeur. Yet with the rise of television as a mass medium, and the resulting competitiveness of Hollywood movies, sexual voyeurism was inevitable. Holroyd could not single-handedly, let alone single-volumely, buck that development. He himself had opened Pandora's box, and he had to live with the consequences.

Holroyd's first intimation that the walls of Jericho were not simply being dismantled but were crashing down came when Nigel Nicolson, one of Holroyd's sternest critics for publishing his original biography of Strachey and thus frightening heirs into destroying evidence, reversed his stance by publishing *Portrait of a Marriage* in 1973. By the end of the 1980s Nicolson had authorized a television dramatization of his parental exposé, starring Janet McTeer and David Haig in the title roles. The writing was clearly on the wall—a projected wall.

Once again, Holroyd adapted his own work. Cutting another quarter of a million words from the original, he retitled his book yet again, as *Lytton Strachey: The New Biography* (1994), to accompany a film that was being made. "The miracle which I am attempting to bring off is the creation of a comparatively shorter book with much more in it," he prefaced his third version of his story.[11] The movie based on Holroyd's work, however, bore the title *Carrington*—Dora Carrington being the focus of the film, written by the playwright Christopher Hampton and starring Jonathan Pryce and Emma Thompson.

Wincing, the last survivors of Bloomsbury now prepared themselves for yet another public scandal. But in a Western society confronting the ravages of AIDS, the tale of Carrington and Strachey's platonic love proved a balm—indeed, a new form of homosexual embalming. The movie of Holroyd's book was widely lauded for its decorum. The beautifully acted story of unrequited love won several awards—and was dubbed, with gentle irony, "the ultimate in safe sex."[12]

Two-Way Traffic: Peter Pan

The journey of Holroyd's *Strachey,* from painstaking card-indexed research to the big screen, was emblematic of biography's development in the final decades of the twentieth century. But the journey could go both ways. Not only was the renaissance of biography being shaped and stimulated by the demands of television and the silver screen, but biographers were often becoming professional writers and directors for television, theater, and Hollywood.

Let's take but one example. J. M. Barrie, author of the Peter Pan plays and novels, had for decades attracted the attention of print biographers—none of whom dared to question the sexuality of the man who had created some of the best-loved children's stories of all time. Barrie had adored actresses, yet it was commonly known that he'd failed to consummate his marriage to the actress Mary Ansell, and that he'd never married again. He had reserved his affections for beautiful children.

In 1970 Janet Dunbar, Barrie's fellow (and much younger) Scottish novelist, published a charming print biography of the diminutive writer (he was only five feet tall) entitled *J. M. Barrie: The Man Behind the Image,* in which she explored the nature of Barrie's fantasy world with regard to mother figures. Yet it was clear to Andrew Birkin, an aspiring screenwriter in the mid-1970s, that Dunbar was skirting the most compelling issue: Barrie's interest not so much in actresses as in young boys.

Birkin discovered that Barrie's special interest in the children of a lawyer named Arthur Llewelyn Davies, youngsters he'd met in Kensington Gardens, had become obsessional. Peter Pan, as a character, had first appeared in Barrie's 1902 novel *The Little White Bird,* in which the narrator hears about a boy encountered in Kensington Gardens at night—a little boy who refuses to grow up. Peter Pan subsequently appeared in Barrie's successful stage play *Peter Pan; or, The Boy Who Wouldn't Grow Up,* which premiered in London on December 27, 1904. In 1906 the portion of *The Little White Bird* that featured Peter Pan was published as *Peter Pan in Kensington Gardens,* illustrated by Arthur Rackham. Barrie then adapted the play into the novel *Peter and Wendy* (1911), thereafter usually published as *Peter Pan.*

The Little White Bird is extraordinarily revealing. Told in the first person, the novel includes an astonishing description of the narrator's emotions as he undresses a little boy named David at bedtime:

> I knew by intuition that he expected me to take off
> his boots. I took them off with all the coolness of an

old hand, and then I placed him on my knee and removed his blouse. This was a delightful experience,
but I think I remained wonderfully calm until I came
somewhat too suddenly to his little braces, which agitated me profoundly. I cannot proceed in public with
the disrobing of David.

David later comes to the narrator's bed.

"Why, David," said I, sitting up, "do you want to
come into my bed?" "Mother said I wasn't to want it
unless you wanted it first," he squeaked. "It is what I
have been wanting all the time," said I, and without
more ado the little figure arose and flung himself at
me. For the rest of the night he lay on me and across
me, and sometimes his feet were at the bottom of
the bed and sometimes on the pillow, but he always
retained possession of my finger. . . . I lay thinking of
this little boy, who, in the midst of his play while I un-
dressed him, had suddenly buried his head on my
knees. . . . Of David's dripping little form in the bath,
and how I essayed to catch him as he slipped from
my arms like a trout. Of how I had stood at the open
door listening to his sweet breathing, had stood so
long I forgot his name. [13]

Edwardian readers had shown no qualms about the homoerotic suggestiveness of Barrie's novel; indeed, in an age when pedophilia was institutionalized at most British private schools and orphanages, such suggestiveness was considered delightful. Certainly the parents of the Kensington boys did not object. Through his platonic courting of Arthur Llewelyn Davies' wife, Sylvia, Barrie (whose writings were making him wealthy) had become deeply and legitimately intimate with Arthur and Sylvia's five children. In 1908, the boys' father died of cancer. Meanwhile, Barrie's own wife, Mary, divorced him for his inability or unwillingness to consummate their marriage. Two years later, Sylvia likewise died of cancer. All five Davies boys—Peter, John, Michael, Nicholas, and Arthur—were legally left in Barrie's care.

Like Charles Dodgson (Lewis Carroll), Barrie took many nude photographs of the boys as they grew to puberty—a fact which made his life story alarmingly "indelicate," yet also more and more intriguing as sexual candor became, thanks to Holroyd and others, prized in biography. Homosexuality between consenting adults was no longer grounds for criminal prosecution. Pedophilia, involving children too young to give legal consent, raised far more perplexing concerns.

Andrew Birkin's later account of what happened is revealing, since it demonstrates how amateur and haphazard the *process* of biography can still be—reflecting as it does the often unpredictable intersections among audience, market, commissioning agencies, owners of evidence, and the sheer individual fascination, even obsession, of one individual who wishes to tell the story of another, ostensibly on behalf of us all.

Birkin's connection with the Barrie saga went back to childhood. Not only had he been a reader of *Peter Pan,* but in the 1920s his mother had sung "The Peter Pan Song" to accompany the silent film version of *Peter Pan* in her husband's cinema in Wales. In 1976 Birkin, as a self-confessed "hack writer," collaborated on an adaptation of a new *Peter Pan* for NBC television's "Hallmark Hall of Fame" series in America—a film which featured Birkin's idol Mia Farrow as Peter, and Danny Kaye as Captain Hook. Birkin served as the "resident Barrie expert" for the production, while Mia Farrow swung and sang above him in the foliage.

Intrigued by the story-behind-the-Barrie-story, a friendly film director, Richard Loncraine, saw dramatic possibilities in what Birkin told him of Barrie's private life, and urged Birkin to write it down. "By the end of shooting I'd skimmed a couple of biographies (notably Janet Dunbar's excellent *J. M. Barrie: The Man behind the Image*) and set about cobbling together an outline that took a good deal of dramatic licence, but was nevertheless a framework on which to hang the story as a film for television," Birkin later recalled. He sent it to the BBC, which commissioned him to write a screenplay—the new producer's first drama. "It was at this point that Sharon Goode, my amazing researcher, tracked down Nico Llewelyn Davies [the fifth of the Llewelyn sons], then living in happy retirement in the countryside. This precipitated a spate of letter writing— over six hundred between the three of us—as well as frequent Sunday visits to his home in Kent."[14]

Nico Llewelyn Davies showed Birkin a trunkful of photos, letters, and memorabilia—including the manuscript of a memoir, entitled "The Morgue," that his brother Peter had written before committing suicide. It was this disturbing new evidence that underpinned Birkin's determination to write not just a ninety-minute television play based on the story, but also a completely original multipart biographical opus for the small screen. "Instead of ninety minutes, I felt we needed four or five hours if we were to tell the story without resorting to the simplified characters and dramatic licence of Hollywood biopics. Louis [the BBC's commissioning producer, Louis Marks] listened patiently. It would mean losing our green-lighted production dates, with no guarantee that in a year's time the whole BBC regime might not have changed for the worse. To my eternal gratitude, Louis agreed to a trilogy totalling four-and-a-half hours."[15]

Having completed his three-part script, *The Lost Boys,* Birkin found himself in the same situation Holroyd had experienced a decade before. Without quite intending to, he had presented a radically fresh take on human (and peculiarly British) sexuality, as he charted Barrie's homo-erotic journey. Birkin's miniseries was considered so far "beyond the pale," and so lengthy, that it was never shown in America.

The successful commissioning of Birkin's BBC series, starring Ian Holm, led to a Holroyd situation in reverse. Whereas Holroyd had been approached by scriptwriter after scriptwriter to adapt the Strachey-Carrington story *for* the screen, Birkin was soon pressed to adapt his screenplay *from* the screen into a book.

Birkin originally intended to be conventional—in fact, simply to "to edit Peter Davies' 'Morgue,'" he recalled. "But Nico felt that it would require far too many foot-notes" to make it understandable. Since film and television writers commonly use researchers, Birkin wondered if Sharon Goode was interested in tackling the job. "Sharon was either too modest or too wise to write a biography herself, so I took the plunge."[16]

Again, the very naïveté of the biographical endeavor, after centuries of biographical history, is telling. Birkin says the following in the third edition of his book, published by Yale University Press in 2003:

> The publishers Constable agreed to take it, believing it to be some sort of TV tie-in of so-many-thousand words. The finished typescript ended up over twice the contractual length. After a good deal of haggling, a 300-page limit was agreed upon, and a hundred pages chopped, which meant I had to end the saga somewhat abruptly at Michael's death in 1921. [This was the first edition, published by Constable in 1979.] A second edition in 1986 allowed me to add new material in the margins without disturbing the original pagination, and this third edition permits the same. But it still leaves a wealth of material unpublished, not to mention the many new things that have turned up in the intervening years. These include all Barrie's original notes for *Peter Pan*—over 700, long believed lost—which I discovered in the Beinecke Library at Yale in the 1980s, and spent many weeks transcribing from Barrie's microscopic scrawl. What makes these notes so remarkable is the realisation that Barrie wrote his first draft of the play without any mention of Captain Hook at all. He didn't need a

villain because he already had one: "P[eter] a demon boy (villain of story)." It was only due to the prosaic necessity of a "front-cloth scene" to give the stage-hands time to change the scenery from the Never Never Land back to the Darling Nursery that Hook was conceived at all.[17]

The dramatic artist, in other words, had become not only a pioneer of televised biography but—through the process of television research, in the least expected way—a pioneering print biographer, too.

The Blurring of the Lines

By the 1980s and '90s, television was awash in biographical dramas—movies starring Edward Fox as King Edward VIII in *Edward and Mrs. Simpson* (1978), Malcolm Stoddard as Darwin in *The Voyage of the Beagle* (1980), Anthony Hopkins as Hitler in *The Bunker* (1981), Ingrid Bergman as Golda Meir in *A Woman Named Golda* (1982), Jean Stapleton as Eleanor Roosevelt in *Eleanor* (1982), Richard Burton as Richard Wagner in *Wagner* (1983), Warren Mitchell as FDR in *The Last Bastion* (1984), Michael Gambon as Oscar Wilde in *Forbidden Passion* (1987), Joe Don Baker as Roy Cohn in *Citizen Cohn* (1992), and Philip Casnoff as Frank Sinatra in *Sinatra* (1992). The sheer power of these films was profoundly influencing life depiction—indeed, it quickly began to spill over from drama into television documentary film, launching a vogue for dramatized segments *within* documentary films. Epitomized by London Weekend Television's series *The Modern World: Ten Great Writers* (1988), such partly dramatized documentaries have become almost *de rigueur.* The upshot was that, whether in poetry, novels, radio, film, or television drama, the blurring of the lines between fiction and nonfiction became, as Marjorie Garber has noted, a "fact" of postmodern reality.[18]

In style and presentation, modern biographers were clearly learning to borrow from their fiction-writing counterparts when it came to narrative, coloration, and technique. Their work abounded in flashbacks, close-ups, varying points of view, and narrative tropes that were subject only to the relative indulgence of an increasingly sophisticated modern biographical (and graphically savvy) audience. Conversely, novelists were borrowing techniques from documentary biographies. But what of the human *victims* of such diverse and often speculative insights into a life story? People could get hurt by the very invasiveness of modern, no-holds-barred biography, as Dora Carrington's brother had pointed out. This issue came to the forefront with Janet Malcolm's elegiac narrative of the injustices committed against Ted Hughes, the husband of Sylvia Plath, a story first told in a series of articles Malcolm wrote for the *New Yorker* magazine. Published in book form as *The Silent Woman* in 1994, it went to the very heart of biography's late twentieth-century dilemma.

Prometheus' Liver

In researching her account of the Plath-Hughes Wars, Janet Malcolm's feminist heart had, paradoxically, gone out not to Sylvia Plath, but to Plath's husband, the English poet laureate, who had been forced to live a life of unending public speculation and feminist vilification following Plath's suicide in 1963.

"Like Prometheus, whose ravaged liver was daily reconstituted so it could be daily reravaged," Malcolm wrote in her seminal attack on intrusive contemporary biography, Ted Hughes "has had to watch his young self [that is, the person he was while married to Sylvia Plath] being picked over by biographers, scholars, critics, article writers, and newspaper journalists." Whose life *was* it, anyway? As a biographer, critic, essayist, and journalist, Malcolm was ashamed. "Biography," she declared, "is the medium through which the remaining secrets of the famous dead are taken from them and dumped out in full view of the

The Silent Woman

Sylvia Plath & Ted Hughes

Janet Malcolm

'Completely brilliant'
David Hare

world. The biographer at work, indeed, is like the professional burglar, breaking into a house, rifling through certain drawers that he has good reason to think contain the jewelry and money, and triumphantly bearing his loot away." If biography had become the most popular form of nonfiction writing, it was not because biographies "teach people how to regard themselves, how to make themselves intelligible to each other, and how to conduct themselves, and their destiny," as one distinguished student of biography maintained.[19] Rather, according to Malcolm, it is biography's "transgressive nature" that is "the only explanation for biography's status as a popular genre. The reader's amazing tolerance (which he would extend to no novel written half as badly as most biographies) makes sense only when seen as a kind of collusion between him and the biographer in an excitingly forbidden undertaking: tiptoeing down the corridor together, to stand in front

---

19. Journalism had always provided the rough draft for history. As the twentieth century came to a close, it began to do so for biography also. Janet Malcolm's *New Yorker* magazine articles investigating the chroniclers and interpreters of poet Sylvia Plath—their motives, the victimization of Plath's husband, and the nature of postmodern biography—became a seminal book, *The Silent Woman*, in 1994. *Jacket photo; reproduced by kind permission of Granta.*

of the bedroom door and try to peep through the key-hole."[20]

Malcolm's stirring defense of her subject—a man she never met—was nobly intended, coming as it did after her bruising at the hands of another man, psychoanalyst Jeffrey Moussaieff Masson, projects director of the Freud Archives. (Masson had sued her for $1 million after her book *Inside the Freud Archives* was published in 1991—claiming that Malcolm, in order to skewer him, had fabricated extensive and embarrassing quotations from the interviews he'd given her.)[21] Notwithstanding this, Malcolm became determined to vindicate Hughes's right to privacy.

The Silent Woman was by far the most brilliant exposé of the workings of modern biography, as well as an eloquent attack on biography's ghoulish popularity, written in the final decade of the twentieth century. Yet Malcolm's defense of the privacy of the English widower proved, in the end, unnecessary. Hoarding poem after poem that he penned about his earlier life with Sylvia, Hughes was content to let his sister Olwyn be his agent in handling the copyrights he had inherited from Sylvia (who had been about to divorce him), and to meanwhile get on with his own promiscuous and prolific life as a poet, children's-story writer, and translator. Then, as he lay dying of cancer in 1998, he took his poems from their secret hiding place, and, to the consternation of Janet Malcolm and millions of others, broke his much-vaunted silence on the subject of his former wife. Under the title *Birthday Letters*, he gave the world his own version of his courtship of Plath, their absolute devotion to the muse of poetry, their wild marriage, their proud parenting, Sylvia's always tenuous hold on sanity, their traumatic breakup, her awful suicide. And the pain of posterity.

In the penultimate poem of the volume, Hughes warned his grown-up daughter about the "dogs"—the press, the media, the feminists who hated him for his craggy handsomeness and sexual magnetism, as well as for his blatant adultery with another woman, which had cost Sylvia, an intensely passionate and jealous individual, her fragile hold on life.

> *Protect her*
> *And they will tear you down*
> *As if you were more of her.*
> *They will find you every bit*
> *As succulent as she is . . .*[22]

Having robbed the grave, the dogs had gorged upon her body, even chipped his name (her married name) from her headstone. They wewe welcome, though, to hump and vomit over their literary dissections.

The victim of biography got his revenge, in biographical verse. And with Hughes's *Birthday Letters* and his own passing, the century—biography's richest and most extraordinary—was over.

CHAPTER 13

Biography Today

I n its historic role as record-keeper of the individual, biography thus moved to the forefront of Western culture at the end of the twentieth century. By 2000 it was represented in almost every field of human inquiry, of communications, and of academic study. Samuel Johnson's vision had been fulfilled; in fact, as the third millennium got under way it was clear to all but the most myopic that biography had become the most popular, and in many ways the most controversial and contested, area of nonfiction broadcasting and publishing in the Western world[1]—epitomized by today's burgeoning weblogs, online diaries in which individuals' thoughts and experiences are published in electronic form. Students of English literature and creative writing are studying and composing more biographical and autobiographical texts than fictional ones;[2] sociology students have jettisoned a seventy-year bias against qualitative as opposed to quantitative research in looking at "society";[3] and in film schools, biographical and autobiographical projects outnumber fictional works.

How, then, can the term "biography" remain today so limited in its definition, and the history of biography as a basic feature of Western civilization remain so neglected and marginalized at most universities in the world?[4] How, in an age when new university disciplines have been established for the study of women's history, black history, sports history, popular culture, hip-hop, journalism, and myriad other aspects of modern culture, is it possible that there could be no school of biography, and only a single major university department in the entire world (Hawaii) devoted to the history, theory, and praxis of the subject, with its own interdisciplinary journal?[5] In an age in which individual human identity has become the focus of so much discussion, and reality TV and blogging so dominate Western culture, how is it possible to go on ignoring biography's long history and its current *significance* in the West?

Old prejudices die hard, and not everyone welcomes, even in the liberal West, the rise of the real alongside the virtual. *New York Times* book critic Michiko Kakutani has given vent to the perplexity and distaste of many literary commentators in the face of today's permeable boundaries between fact and fiction:

> We live in a relativistic culture where television "reality shows" are staged or stage-managed, where spin sessions and spin doctors are an accepted part of politics, where academics argue that history depends on who is writing the history. Phrases like "virtual reality" and "creative nonfiction" have become part of our language. Hype and hyperbole are an accepted part of marketing and public relations. And reinvention and repositioning are regarded as useful career moves in the worlds of entertainment and politics. The conspiracy-minded, fact-warping movies of Oliver Stone are regarded by those who don't know better as genuine history, as are the most sensationalistic of television docudramas.[6]

In her eyes, the representation of the "real" has become an unpleasant and meretricious spectacle, its fall from grace epitomized by reports that a vivid new best-selling autobiography by James Frey, entitled *A Million Little Pieces*, comprised many pieces of pure fiction.

Kakutani laments the fact that "objective" and "subjective" are not well delineated in today's media. But this lack of delineation is not really news. "That biography—and even more, autobiography—is a species of fiction-making is a truth so old that only willed cultural amnesia can make it new," Marjorie Garber wrote a decade ago, correcting those who hold rigid views on what is and is not permissible.[7] The rest, Garber pointed out, is up to us, the audience. The very freedom to fabricate is accompanied, in the West, by the freedom too contest—and to expose. Oliver Stone's fantasies have been revealed by innumerable biographers and historians, thanks to the freedom of speech enjoyed by Western artists and academics. James Frey's mendacity, too, was uncovered in due course.

Distressed by its tackier manifestations—particularly the pandering to a culture of celebrity, all too many critics overlook the very *importance* of biography in modern Western democracy, and ignore the extent to which the best life depiction has improved since World War II, in response to modern (or postmodern) times. Irreverent, humorous, often tabloid but endlessly curious about individuality, the sum of biographical output is a tribute to the diversity of modern Western democracy. As Paula Backscheider pointed out in 1999, "Any art that becomes mass culture, as biography has done with television, magazines and numbers of

new book series, carries heavy cultural weight." To overlook its role in modern communications and society is a
serious mistake, in her view, for modern biography "can
penetrate or create new myths about the men and women
that a nation's people imitate or scorn."[8] We have seen
how, since Lytton Strachey, the task of challenging myths
has become a *sine qua non* of modern biography. Biographers accept that no single definitive account of a human
life is possible, yet are aware that they are part of a wave of
insistent attempts, highbrow *and* lowbrow, to reinterpret
past and present lives on behalf of the current generation—the better, on the whole, to understand those lives,
not to retail propaganda, as in a dictatorship.

Such freedom, which extends to the millions of individuals who read and view biographical work, is as much a
measure of democratic reality as parliamentary government.

In the cultural arena, biography also dominates the
twenty-first-century stage, inverting the Victorian fiction–
fact paradigm. It may be said, in fact, that biography has
largely changed places with fiction. Where once factual
biographical reporting seemed hard and certain, while fiction could be dismissed as "make-believe," the roles are
now reversed. As Janet Malcolm put it already in 1994, the
many contradictory, contested "facts" of the Plath-Hughes

story underscore the "epistemological insecurity by which the reader of biography and autobiography (and history and journalism) is always and everywhere dogged. In a work of non-fiction we almost never know the truth of what happened." By contrast, the "ideal of unmediated reporting is regularly achieved in fiction, where the writer faithfully reports on what is going on in his imagination. . . . Only in non-fiction does the question of what happened and how people thought and felt remain open."[9]

Open—and, thankfully, debated in our society. Formerly the "mealy-mouthed" journeymen of Victorian letters, the practitioners of biography and autobiography have, in sum, journeyed to the edge of a new universe and, to their own surprise, have furnished us with one of the most contested, challenging, and endlessly fascinating areas of contemporary book publishing, film, television, radio broadcasting, theater, and Internet activity.

Reading Other People's Mail

Seen in this larger perspective, the adaptive, evolutionary cross-fertilization between biography and fiction clearly inspires *both* pursuits, at every level, and in every medium. Not everyone welcomed this. Janet Malcolm, for example, expressly attacked the underlying hypocrisy that was keeping biography afloat, behind a mask of modern biographical "scholarship":

> The voyeurism and busybodyism that impel writers and readers of biography alike are obscured by an apparatus of scholarship designed to give the enterprise an appearance of blanklike blandness and solidarity. The biographer is portrayed almost as a kind of benefactor. He is seen as sacrificing years of his life to his task, tirelessly sitting in archives and libraries and patiently conducting interviews and witnesses. There is no length he will not go to, and the more his book reflects his industry the more he believes that he is having an elevating literary experience, rather than simply listening to backstairs gossip and reading other people's mail.[10]

Given that Ms. Malcolm had never actually sacrificed years of her life to a seriously researched scholarly biography, this was, to say the least, unfair. Indisputably, the sheer research endeavor and scholarship of many late twentieth-century biographers has enormously enriched the learning-base of Western society.[11] These include Richard Holmes, Deirdre Bair, Bernard Crick, Leslie A. Marchand, Martin

Gilbert, Joseph Ellis, Alan Massie, Doris Kearns Goodwin, Humphrey Carpenter, Victoria Glendinning, Lyndall Gordon, Hermione Lee, Judith Brown, Philip Ziegler, Brenda Maddox, H. C. Robbins, and many *thousands* of others.

In turn, the profusion of scholarly, deeply researched print biographies has encouraged many novelists to do more careful research when incorporating real individuals in their fictional work. Thus, for example, Philip Roth's brilliant book *The Plot against America* would have proven a far less convincing speculative fiction on the threat to Jews in America in the 1940s during the administration of the fictional "President Lindbergh," had the author not read a number of biographical accounts of the pioneer aviator and political appeaser Charles Lindbergh—a debt that Roth acknowledges at the end of his novel. From Norman Mailer's *Marilyn* (1973) to Colm Toíbín's *The Master* (2004)—through A. S. Byatt's *Possession,* Joe Eszterhas' *American Rhapsody,* Alain de Botton's *Kiss and Tell,* and David Lodge's *Henry James*—novelists have toyed with, and will continue to toy with, the realm of biography in an age dominated by the stories and storytelling of real individuals. As books and television dramatizations beget more small- and big-screen biopics—such as Jan Schütte's *Abschied* (The Farewell; 2002, starring Josef Bierbichler), a haunting portrait of Bertolt Brecht and his circle of women; or Oliver Hirschbiegel's *Der Untergang* (The Downfall; 2004, starring Bruno Ganz), a dramatized depiction, based on Joachim Fest's print biography and Traudl Junge's documentary film interview, of Hitler's last days—it is obvious that even if lexicographers remain stuck in the nineteenth century, writers, artists, directors, and reference-book compilers have entered the twenty-first. *The Biography Book* by Daniel Burt, published in 2001, is perhaps the best marker of this turning-point in biography's fortunes. A reference compendium for high-profile biography, it lists not only nonfiction works on individual lives in print, but also "Biographical Novels" and "Biographical Films and Theatrical Adaptations."[12]

Making Sense of Your Life

The truth is that real-life depiction—in myriad forms, from comic strip[13] to essay, from obituaries to dramatized TV epics, from films to operas, from museum exhibitions to books, from radio profiles to film documentaries and blogs—is today the mark of our continuing fascination with individuality. However much we may mock the exhibitionism which TV programs such as the *Jerry Springer Show* encourage, or the plethora of narcissistic blogs on the Internet, there can be no denying people's urge to be

heard as individuals and not merely as faceless statistics or members of voting blocs.

William Zinsser articulated this desire very well in 2006, when he was called upon to address the significance of the Frey scandal and the truth-in-memoir issues it raised. (Forced to admit, in public, that much of his best-selling life story was fabricated, the hapless Frey had been lambasted by the talk-show host Oprah Winfrey, who, like hundreds of thousands of readers, felt betrayed by Frey's autobiographical deception.) Deploring the "torrent of memoirs that wallowed in self-pity and self-revelation" in the 1990s—the "decade of the memoir," as he called it[14]— Zinsser did, however, express sympathy for those *attempting* the autobiographical journey.

---

20. Comic-strip "novels" (books) provided yet another artistic channel for biographical work in the late twentieth century, which saw accelerated interbreeding among traditional biographical forms, norms, and media. Harvey Pekar made his name in the 1970s with *American Splendor,* an autobiographical comic book that recorded the mundane real life of a hospital file clerk. Decades later, it was the inspiration for countless blogs. Here, a poster advertises the 2003 dramatized biography of Pekar's life, starring Paul Giamatti—and featuring, in interposed scenes, the real Harvey Pekar. *American Splendor* © *2003, New Line Films, Inc. All rights reserved. Poster appears courtesy of New Line Productions, Inc.*

> For many years I've been teaching adult courses in memoir writing and family history at the New School and elsewhere, and it occurs to me that the writing teacher, without signing up for it, has become one of the country's listeners, joining the therapist and the priest and the rabbi. People turn up for writing classes, and they look so together, they are nicely dressed, they have been organized enough in their life to sign up for the course and to be in the right place at the right time. Then they begin to talk about the stories they want to write, and you realize that they are struggling with a tremendous residue of adversity, which you would not otherwise know about.

Zinsser is not a psychotherapist, and says he has no wish to become one. What he believes he can provide is help in explaining "a mechanism whereby you will try to make sense of your life."[15]

Film mentors have similar experiences. For example, by the time the documentary filmmaker Richard P. Rogers died in 2001, at age fifty-seven, he had amassed *150 hours* of autobiographical film, both mentoring material and self-observation.[16]

Zinsser's adult students, meanwhile, were "using writing to come to some understanding of who they are, and who they once were, and what heritage they were born into. I'm struck by the courage and honesty with which my students are trying to accomplish that." James Frey might be "running away from the truth, but I don't think that's what most writers of memoir are aiming for. I think they are desperately trying to use writing to find the truth about their lives."[17]

To which one can only add: Amen. Like the painted images on late Egyptian mummies, the myriad biographical depictions we are producing today—artistic and inartistic, noble and tacky—will form the record we leave of ourselves to posterity. This alone surely means that biography's history and praxis are worth further study—and, as the third millennium gets under way, makes a redefinition of "biography" long overdue.

Epilogue

Today, biography is in the ascendant. But before we leave the subject, let's look briefly into the future of life depiction, however misty our lens.

So massively popular an outflow of works reflecting society's fascination with the individual is likely to continue to grow exponentially in the West. Yet just as biographers in the 1920s wondered whether dictatorship would lead to renewed hagiography (which it did), one wonders what might happen if *individuality* itself is superseded—as the result, say, of a political or religious ideology (communism or Islam), or of scientific advances that alter the biological nature of human individuality.

The latter scenario is closer than one might imagine. After Dolly the sheep was cloned on July 5, 1996, by scientists at the Roslin Institute, Edinburgh, the concept of individuality—the very basis of Western civilization since the Renaissance—became not only a contested issue, but, literally, tissue.

Dolly died young, at age six—put to sleep by her creators after developing a progressive lung disease. Genetic cloning, however, has continued—and will inevitably be performed with humans, not simply with plants and animals. Genetic alterations *after* birth will likewise affect individuality, now that the human genome has been mapped and human "defects" can be modified or "corrected."

What task will biography assume as the depictor of real individuals, once individuality comes to be altered, standardized, and "processed"? The future is intriguing not simply to science fiction writers but to those of us who love biography as the study of the individual.

There's no telling how real-life depiction will continue to develop, once cloning becomes widespread. This will be a new chapter in the unending life-or-death struggle, as it were, of Biography. Meanwhile, the study of evolutionary psychology—the heated debate over nature versus nurture, the argument over genetic predisposition versus the civilizing imperatives of Western society—has made the business of real-life depiction in the modern world all the more engaging, and controversial.

As a species, we still enjoy many of the characteristics of our cousins, the apes, while perpetually inventing new ways of thinking and doing as individual humans. As the primatologist Frans de Waal has written, cloning may be intellectually exciting as a potentially better way to reproduce, by capitalizing on proven genes "without mixing in the imperfections of somebody else's genes." Yet that very mixing is the feature that has allowed our species to survive thus far. Besides, de Waal has pointed out, it would mark the end of biography as the expression of our curiosity about individuals. "Imagine the brave new world we would inhabit, full of genderless, identical-looking individuals. No more gossip about who loves whom, who divorces whom, or who cheats on whom." No more "sins of the flesh, but also no infatuation, no romantic movies, and no pop star sex symbols. It might be more efficient, but it would also be the most boring place one can imagine."[1]

Notes

PROLOGUE

1. Center for Biographical Research, University of Hawaii at Manoa. See www.hawaii.edu/biograph (accessed September 2006). For a discussion of the academic antibiographical stance (despite the increasing numbers of biographers writing today), see Paula R. Backscheider, *Reflections on Biography* (Oxford: Oxford University Press, 1999), p. xx.

CHAPTER I. EVOLUTIONARY BIOGRAPHY

1. André Leroi-Gourhan, *Treasures of Prehistoric Art* (New York: Harry N. Abrams, 1963), pp. 121ff.
2. Describing the mummy portraits found in the tombs at El Rabayat, Egypt, displayed at the British Museum's *Ancient Faces* exhibition in 1997, Susan Walker remarked on the "keen sense of individuality: skin tone, facial hair and bone structure are meticulously recorded and, within the corpus, considerably varied"—serving as "a record of the deceased as he or she had appeared in life." See Susan Walker and Morris Bierbrier, *Ancient Faces: Mummy Portraits from Roman Egypt* (London: British Museum Press, 1997), pp. 15 and 14.
3. See Duane Reed Stuart, *Epochs of Greek and Roman Biography* (New York: Biblo and Tannen, 1967; orig. pub. 1928), p. 9.
4. Ibid., p. 10.
5. Ibid., p. 129.
6. *Life of Timoleon*, in Plutarch, *The Age of Alexander,* trans. Ian Scott-Kilvert (Harmondsworth: Penguin, 1973), p. 151.

7. *Life of Alexander,* ibid., p. 252.

8. "Biography," in *Encyclopaedia Britannica* (Cambridge: Cambridge University Press, 1910).

9. Xenophon, *The Education of Cyrus,* trans. H. G. Dakyns (London: Dent, Everyman Edition, 1992; orig. pub. 1914), p. 4.

10. *Life of Alexander,* in Plutarch, *The Age of Alexander,* p. 252.

11. Ibid.

12. Suetonius, *The Twelve Caesars,* trans. Robert Graves, revised by Michael Grant (Harmondsworth: Penguin, 1979; orig. pub. 1957), p. 34.

CHAPTER 2. HAGIOGRAPHY

1. Paul Murray Kendall, "Biography," in *Encyclopaedia Britannica* (1974).

2. Paul Murray Kendall, *The Art of Biography* (London: Allen and Unwin, 1965), pp. 32–33.

3. See, inter alia, Elaine Pagels, *The Gnostic Gospels* (New York: Vintage, 1979).

4. See James J. O'Donnell, *Augustine: The New Biography* (New York: Ecco, 2005). Also O'Donnell's webpage "Augustine of Hippo," at www.georgetown.edu/faculty/jod/augustine (accessed September 2006).

5. Saint Augustine, *Confessions,* trans. R. S. Pine-Coffin (Harmondsworth: Penguin, 1961), p. 55.

6. Peter Calvocoressi, *Who's Who in the Bible* (London: Viking, 1987), p. 11.

7. Reed Whittemore, *Pure Lives: The Early Biographers* (Baltimore: Johns Hopkins University Press, 1988), p. 43.

8. It should be noted that hagiography, in the wake of recent trends in sociology, history, and literary studies, has begun to enjoy renewed interest in academia, spawning a growing number of scholarly reconsiderations of the "Dark Ages" and their individual life histories.

9. Saint Augustine, *Confessions,* p. 102.

CHAPTER 3. THE RENAISSANCE OF BIOGRAPHY

1. Jacob Burckhardt, *The Civilization of the Renaissance in Italy,* trans. S. G. C. Middlemore (New York: Random House, Modern Library, 1954), p. 100. Burckhardt's clear-cut distinction between the Renaissance and the Middle Ages has been challenged, but his essential thesis regarding the flowering of thought, culture, and society in Renaissance Italy remains remarkably potent 150 years after first publication.

2. In *Henry VI, Part I,* Shakespeare included a portrayal of Joan of Arc, but not as a saint.

3. Sir Walter Raleigh, *The History of the World,* ed. C. A. Patrides (Philadelphia: Temple University Press, 1971), p. 48.

4. Ibid., p. 80.

5. Ibid., p. 57.

6. Patrides, Introduction, quoting John Chamberlain to Sir Dudley Carleton, 5 January 1615, in Raleigh, *The History of the World,* p. 11.

7. Sir Thomas Overbury, *The Arraignment and Conviction of Sir Walter Rawleigh* (1648), p. 34.

8. Raleigh, *The History of the World,* p. 80.

9. Ibid.

10. Ibid., p. 68.

11. Ibid., p. 47.

12. Ibid.

13. Ibid.

14. Donald A. Stauffer, *English Biography before 1700* (Cambridge, Mass.: Harvard University Press, 1930), p. 219.

15. See James L. Clifford, *Biography as an Art* (New York: Oxford University Press, 1962), pp. 27–39; and Peter Millard, ed., *Roger North: The General Preface and Life of Dr. John North* (Toronto: University of Toronto Press, 1984); and Roger North, *Notes of Me: The Autobiography of Roger North,* ed. Peter Millard (Toronto: University of Toronto Press, 2000).

16. John Aubrey, *Brief Lives,* ed. Andrew Clark (Oxford: Oxford University Press, 1898), vol. 1, p. 43.

17. Raleigh, *The History of the World,* p. 47.

18. James Boswell, *Boswell's Life of Johnson,* ed. G. H. Hill (Oxford: Oxford University Press, 1934), vol. 3, p. 155.

19. Ibid., vol. 4, p. 53.

20. Samuel Johnson, in *The Rambler,* 60 (October 13, 1750). Roger North, in his general preface to his *Life of the Lord Keeper North,* penned some years earlier but not published until 1962, had expressed a similar sentiment: "The history of private lives adapted to the perusal of common men, is more beneficial (generally) than the most solemn registers of ages, and nations. . . . The gross reason is, because the latter contain little if any thing, comparate or comparable to instruct a private economy, or tending to make a man either wiser or more cautelous [sic], in his own proper concerns." Quoted in Clifford, *Biography as an Art,* p. 27.

21. Johnson, in *The Rambler,* 60 (October 13, 1750).

22. Ibid.

23. Ibid.

24. Oliver Goldsmith, quoted in Boswell, *Boswell's Life of Johnson,* vol. 5, p. 79.

25. Sir Walter Raleigh, *Six Essays on Johnson* (Oxford: Oxford University Press, 1910), p. 117.

26. Richard D. Altick, *Lives and Letters: A History of Literary Biography in England and America* (New York: Knopf, 1966), pp. 73–74.

27. Michel de Montaigne, *Essays,* trans. Donald M. Frame (Palo Alto: Stanford University Press, 1958), p. 503.

28. Jean-Jacques Rousseau, trans. anonymous, *The Confessions* (Ware, U.K.: Wordsworth Editions, 1996), p. 583.

CHAPTER 4. VICTORIAN PSEUDOBIOGRAPHY

1. Sir Walter Scott, "Scott's Unfinished Autobiography," in Randall Gibbons, comp., *In Their Own Words* (New York: Random House, 1995), p. 335.

2. First published in 1830 in Palmyra, New York, *The Book of Mormon* was the work of Joseph Smith, founder of the Church of Jesus Christ of Latter-Day Saints, in Utah. Smith's miraculous revelation concerned a group of Jews who supposedly migrated to America from Jerusalem about 600 B.C., led by a prophet, Lehi. These Jews multiplied and eventually split into two groups. One group, the Lamanites, forgot their beliefs, became heathens, and were the ancestors of the American Indians. The other group, the Nephites, developed culturally and built great cities. Jesus had appeared in their presence and ministered to them, after his Resurrection and Ascension. The Nephites were nevertheless eventually destroyed by the Lamanites about 400 A.D. Only when a resurrected prophet, Moroni, delivered the history and teachings—abridged and written on gold plates by his father, the prophet Mormon—to Joseph Smith (who subsequently returned them to Moroni) was the secret history revealed, but no evidence was ever offered, or has been found, to validate the account.

3. A. O. J. Cockshut, *The Art of Autobiography in Nineteenth- and Twentieth-Century England* (New Haven: Yale University Press, 1984), p. 31.

4. André Maurois, *Aspects of Biography* (New York: D. Appleton, 1929), p. 82.

5. Paul Murray Kendall, *The Art of Biography* (London: Allen and Unwin, 1965), p. 102.

6. Thomas De Quincey, *Confessions of an English Opium Eater* (London, 1821).

7. Harold Nicolson, *The Development of English Biography* (London: Hogarth, 1927).

8. See, inter alia, John Powell, ed., *Victorian Biography,* special issue of *Nineteenth-Century Prose,* 22, no. 2 (Fall 1995). Also Ira Bruce Nadel, *Biography: Fiction, Fact, and Form* (New York: St. Martin's, 1984).

9. Casanova's *Histoire de ma vie* was first published in a translated German edition in twenty-eight volumes in 1822–1828, then in a bowdlerized French edition in 1838, then in a similarly bowdlerized, inac-

curate English translation by Arthur Machen in 1894. An accurate version of the French original was not published until 1960, followed by the first complete English edition, translated by W. R. Trask, in six volumes (1966–1971). The filmography of Casanova's autobiography, however, reveals far less inhibition, from silent film through talkies and television: *Casanova* (1918, Hungary), dir. Alfréd Deésy, starring Alfréd Deésy; *Casanova: The Loves of Casanova* (1927, France), dir. Alexandre Volkoff, starring Ivan Mosjoukine; *Casanova* (1928, Germany), starring Michael Bohnen; *Casanova* (1934, France), dir. René Barberis, starring Ivan Mosjoukine; *Aventures de Casanova*, a.k.a. *Loves of Casanova* (1947, France), dir. Jean Boyer, starring Georges Guetary; *Adventures of Casanova* (1948, U.S.), dir. Roberto Gavaldón, starring Arturo De Cordova; *Casanova '70* (1965, France/Italy), dir. Mario Monicelli, starring Marcello Mastroianni; *Infanzia, vacazione e prime experienze di Casanova Veneziano* (1969, Italy), dir. Luigi Comencini, starring Claudio De Kunert and Leonard Whiting; *Casanova* (1971, U.K., television serial), dir. Mark Cullingham and John Glenister, starring Frank Finlay; *Fellini's Casanova* (1976, Italy), dir. Federico Fellini, starring Donald Sutherland; *Casanova & Co.* (1977, Germany), dir. Franz Antel, starring Tony Curtis; *Casanova* (1981, Germany, television film), dir. Kurt Pscherer, starring Walter Koeninger; *Casanova*, a.k.a. *Il Veneziano: Vita e amori di Giacomo Casanova* (1987, U.K., television film), dir. Simon Langton, starring Richard Chamberlain; *Goodbye, Casanova* (2000, U.S.), dir. Mauro Borrelli, starring Gian-Carlo Scandiuzzi; *Casanova* (2004, Germany, television film), dir. Richard Blank, starring Robert Hunger-Bühler; *Casanova* (2005, U.K., television serial), dir. Sheree Folkson, starring Peter O'Toole and David Tennant; *Casanova* (2005, U.S.), dir. Lasse Hallström, starring Heath Ledger.

10. Virginia Woolf, *Orlando: A Biography* (Harmondsworth: Penguin, 1963; orig. pub. 1928), pp. 161–162.

11. William Godwin, *Memoirs of the Author of "A Vindication of the Rights of Woman."* First published in London, 1798.

12. Introduction to J. R. Morgan and Richard Stoneman, eds., *Greek Fiction: The Greek Novel in Context* (London: Routledge, 1994), p. 5.

13. Sir Walter Raleigh, *The History of the World*, ed. C. A. Patrides (Philadelphia: Temple University Press, 1971), p. 48.

14. Lytton Strachey, *Eminent Victorians* (Harmondsworth: Penguin, 1986; orig. pub. 1918), p. 10.

15. Nadel, *Biography: Fiction, Fact, and Form*, p. 72.

16. Ibid., p. 87.

17. D. F. Strauss's *Leben Jesu*.

18. See Ian Hamilton, *Keepers of the Flame: Literary Estates and the Rise of Biography* (London: Hutchinson, 1992), pp. 131–133.

19. Edward Dowden, quoted ibid., p. 137.

20. Ibid., p. 91.

21. See ibid., pp. 128–143.

22. Samuel Smiles, *Life of George Stephenson* (London: J. Murray, 1857), p. 163. The work was published in the United States the following year, and by the 1880s some 60,000 copies were in print. Nadel, *Biography: Fiction, Fact, and Form*, pp. 24 and 214.

23. Quoted in Nadel, *Biography: Fiction, Fact, and Form*, p. 19.

24. Thomas Carlyle, review of J. G. Lockhart, *Memoirs of the Life of Sir Walter Scott, Baronet, Vols. I–VI*, in *London and Westminster Review*, 12 (1838).

CHAPTER 5. THE EARLY TWENTIETH CENTURY

1. Edmund Gosse, "The Custom of Biography," *Anglo-Saxon Review*, 8 (March 1901).

2. The model was Madame Pierre Gautreau, who had a "bad" reputation. "Though Madame Gautreau's adulteries were well known, thanks to gossip and scandal sheets, they were not considered a fit subject for polite conversation. It was unthinkable for a painter to offer emblems of her way of life to audiences at the Salon, that sacrosanct institution of French culture. Yet that is what Sargent did. His painting rendered faithfully her covering of lavender pow-

der, an affectation of the most brazenly voluptuous sort. Moreover, Sargent emphasized the arrogance with which she flaunted
her décolletage." Carter Ratcliff, *John Singer Sargent* (New York:
Cross River Press, 1982).

3. Sigmund Freud, *Dora,* in *The Standard Edition of the Complete Psychological Works of Sigmund Freud,* ed. James Strachey (London:
Hogarth, 1953–1974), vol. 7.

4. Michel Foucault, *The History of Sexuality,* vol. 1 (1976), trans. Robert Hurley (New York: Vintage, 1980), p. 18.

5. Freud, *Dora.*

6. Sigmund Freud, letter to Carl Jung, October 17, 1909, quoted in Peter Gay, *Freud: A Life for Our Time* (New York: Norton, 1988), p. 268.

7. Sigmund Freud, *Leonardo da Vinci and a Memory of His Childhood*
(1910), trans. Alan Tyson, ed. James Strachey (New York: Norton,
1961), p. 37.

8. Quoted in Gay, *Freud,* p. 268.

9. Freud, *Leonardo da Vinci,* p. 92.

10. A. Richard Turner, *Inventing Leonardo* (New York: Knopf, 1993; London: Papermac, 1995), p. 147.

11. Richard D. Altick, *Lives And Letters: A History of Literary Biography in
England and America* (New York: Knopf, 1966), p. 245.

12. Lytton Strachey, *Eminent Victorians* [1918] (Harmondsworth: Penguin, 1986), p. 199.

13. Ibid., p. 266.

14. Altick, *Lives and Letters,* p. 292.

15. Barbara Belfort, *Oscar Wilde: A Certain Genius* (New York: Random
House, 2000), p. 234.

16. Quoted in Michael Holroyd, *Lytton Strachey: The New Biography*
(London: Chatto and Windus, 1994), p. 92.

17. See Richard Perceval Graves, *Robert Graves: The Years with Laura
Riding, 1926–1940* (London: Weidenfeld and Nicolson, 1990).

18. Virginia Woolf, "Old Bloomsbury," reprinted in Woolf, *Moments of
Being,* ed. Jeanne Schulkind (London: Chatto and Windus, for Sussex University Press, 1976), p. 200.

19. Aileen Pippett, *The Moth and the Star: A Biography of Virginia Woolf* (Boston: Little, Brown, 1955), p. 242; *Letters of Virginia Woolf,* ed. Nigel Nicolson (London: Hogarth Press, 1977), vol. 2, p. 429.

20. "The public has no claim to learn any more of my personal affairs," Freud wrote in a 1935 postscript, defending his own (rather than Leonardo's) privacy. He felt he had already been "more open and frank" in his writings than most, and had had "small thanks for it." Sigmund Freud, *An Autobiographical Study,* trans. James Strachey (New York: Norton, 1952; orig. pub. 1935), p. 83.

21. Woolf did, of course, pen another highly successful (and delightful) fictional biography—of a dog! *Flush,* published in 1932, was based on the spaniel given to her by Vita Sackville-West in 1926, and on the love story of Elizabeth Barrett and Robert Browning. See Julia Briggs, *Virginia Woolf: An Inner Life* (New York: Harcourt, 2005), pp. 272–278.

22. William Rubin, *Picasso and Portraiture: Representation and Transformation* (New York: Museum of Modern Art, 1996), p. 13.

23. Henry Miller, *Tropic of Cancer* (New York: Grove, 1961), pp. 1–2.

24. Virginia Woolf, "The New Biography," *New York Herald Tribune Books,* October 16, 1927.

25. Ibid.

26. Virginia Woolf, "The Art of Biography," *Atlantic Monthly,* April 1939.

27. Ibid.

28. Woolf, "The New Biography."

CHAPTER 6. THE RISE OF FILM

1. Charles Musser, *The Emergence of Cinema: The American Screen to 1907* (Berkeley: University of California Press, 1990), p. 78.

2. Ibid.

3. Ibid.

4. Ibid., p. 493.

5. Ibid., p. 78.

6. Quoted, inter alia, in Ronald Bergan, *Sergei Eisenstein: A Life in*

Conflict (Woodstock, N.Y.: Overlook Press / Peter Meyer, 1999), p. 339.

7. See Ephraim Katz, *The Film Encyclopedia* (New York: Harper Perennial, 1998), p. 1159.

8. Ken Kelman, "Propaganda as Vision: Triumph of the Will," *Film Culture* (Spring 1973), quoted in Audrey Salkeld, *A Portrait of Leni Riefenstahl* (London: Cape, 1996), p. 157.

9. Virginia Woolf, "The New Biography," *New York Herald Tribune Books,* October 16, 1927.

10. Harold Nicolson, *The Development of English Biography* (London: Hogarth, 1927), p. 10.

11. Ibid.

12. Nigel Hamilton, *JFK: Reckless Youth* (New York: Random House, 1992), p. 379, and endnote, p. 840.

CHAPTER 7. THE PEOPLE'S WAR

1. Benjamin Disraeli, *Contarini Fleming,* Part I, ch. 23 (1832).

2. Samuel Johnson, in *The Rambler,* 60 (October 13, 1750).

3. Albert Camus, *The Outsider,* trans. Joseph Laredo (Harmondsworth: Penguin, 1983), pp. 118–119.

4. Olivier Todd, *Albert Camus: A Life* (New York: Knopf, 1997), p. 411.

5. Irenaeus, *Libros Quinque Adversus Haereses,* 3.11.9, in Elaine Pagels, *The Gnostic Gospels* (New York: Vintage, 1979), p. 17.

CHAPTER 8. DEATH OF THE AUTHOR

1. V. N. Volosinov (aka M. M. Bakhtin), *Marxism and the Philosophy of Language* [1929] (Cambridge, Mass.: Harvard University Press, 1986), p. 86.

2. Roland Barthes, "The Death of the Author," in Barthes, *Image, Music, Text,* trans. Stephen Heath (New York: Hill and Wang, 1977), p. 148. Originally published in *Aspen,* 5–6 (Fall–Winter 1967), translated by Richard Howard. Heath translation reprinted in John Caughie, ed., *Theories of Authorship: A Reader* (London: Routledge, 1981), p. 213.

3. Michel Foucault, "What Is an Author?" (1969), in Foucault, *Language, Counter-Memory, Practice,* ed. D. F. Bouchard (Oxford: Blackwell, 1977).

4. Christopher Butler, *Postmodernism* (Oxford: Oxford University Press, 2002), p. 42.

5. Marjorie Garber, "Introduction: Postmodernism and the Possibility of Biography," in Mary Rhiel and David Suchoff, eds., *The Seductions of Biography* (New York: Routledge, 1996), pp. 175–177.

6. Alan Sokal, "A Physicist Experiments with Cultural Studies," *Lingua Franca* (May–June 1996): 62–64.

7. Butler, *Postmodernism,* p. 116.

CHAPTER 9. NEW DIRECTIONS

1. Harold Nicolson, *The Development of English Biography* (London: Hogarth, 1927), pp. 154–155.

2. Ibid., p. 157.

3. Julian Barnes, *Flaubert's Parrot* (London: Cape, 1984), p. 38.

4. Ibid., p. 100. Sartre's *L'Idiot de la famille* (1971–1972) was published in English as *The Family Idiot,* trans. Carol Cosman (Chicago: University of Chicago Press, 1981).

5. Barnes, *Flaubert's Parrot,* p. 100.

6. Robert Skidelsky, "Only Connect: Biography and Truth," in Eric Homberger and John Charmley, eds., *The Troubled Face of Biography* (New York: St. Martin's, 1988), p. 3.

7. Ibid., p. 13.

CHAPTER 10. BIOGRAPHY COMES OF AGE

1. George F. Custen, *Bio/Pics: How Hollywood Constructed Public History* (New Brunswick, N.J.: Rutgers University Press, 1992), p. 140.

2. Ibid., p. 141.

3. Ibid.

4. John E. O'Connor, "History in Images / Images in History: Reflections on the Importance of Film and Television Study for an

Understanding of the Past," *American Historical Review,* 93, no. 5 (December 1988): 1201.

5. Custen, *Bio/Pics,* pp. 22–23, 190, 146–147.

6. Ian Wilson, *Jesus: The Evidence* (London: Weidenfeld and Nicolson, 1996), p. 53.

7. Graham Chapman et al., *Monty Python's Life of Brian (of Nazareth)* (London: Eyre Methuen, 1979), pp. 46–47.

8. Harold Nicolson, *The Development of English Biography* (London: Hogarth, 1927), pp. 155–156.

9. Ibid., p. 155.

10. Nigel Nicolson, *Portrait of a Marriage* (London: Weidenfeld and Nicolson, 1973), p. 107.

11. *The Journal of Medical Biography* was started in 1991. Even Nicolson's prediction of "biographies in which psychological development will be traced in all its intricacy and in a manner comprehensible only to the experts" seemed fulfilled when psychoanalysts under Dr. Erik Erikson—following in the footsteps of Sigmund Freud in 1909—made a renewed bid for biographical hegemony, culminating with the Conference on Psychoanalysis and Biography, held in Chicago in 1982.

12. William McKinley Runyan, *Life Histories and Psychobiography: Explorations in Theory and Method* (New York: Oxford University Press, 1984), p. 9.

CHAPTER 11. BIOGRAPHY ON TRIAL

1. *Salinger v. Random House,* 650 F. Supp. 413 (1986). See also www.bc.edu/bc_org/avp/cas/comm/free_speech/salinger.html (accessed September 2006).

2. *Eldred v. Aschcroft,* 537 U.S. (2003), Ct 769 at 801.

3. David Pierce, "A Portrait of the Artist's Troubled Daughter," *New York Times,* November 22, 2003.

4. Eric Homberger and John Charmley, eds., *The Troubled Face of Biography* (New York: St. Martin's, 1998), p. xiv.

5. Edmund Morris, *Dutch: A Memoir of Ronald Reagan* (New York: Random House, 1999).

6. Philippe Lejeune, *Le Pacte Autobiographique* (Paris: Editions du Seuil, 1975).

7. Edmund and Sylvia Morris, conversation with the author, Washington, D.C., January 2001.

CHAPTER 12. THE MINER'S CANARY

1. Michael Holroyd, *Lytton Strachey: The New Biography* (London: Chatto and Windus, 1994), p. xxiii, quoting Kenneth Williams, diary entry for January 13, 1969.

2. Ibid., p. xxii.

3. Ibid., p. xxvii.

4. Ibid., quoting Frances Partridge, March 28, 1966.

5. See, inter alia, Paul Thompson, *The Voice of the Past* (Oxford: Oxford University Press, 1978, 1988).

6. Holroyd, *Lytton Strachey,* p. xvii.

7. Ibid., p. xxv.

8. Ibid., quoting Noel Carrington, letter of December 2, 1968.

9. Lytton Strachey, Preface to *Eminent Victorians* [1918] (Harmondsworth: Penguin, 1986), p. 10.

10. Virginia Woolf, "The Art of Biography," *Atlantic Monthly,* April 1939.

11. Holroyd, *Lytton Strachey,* p. xxxi.

12. Owen Gleiberman, Review of *Carrington,* in *Entertainment Weekly,* November 17, 1995.

13. J. M. Barrie, *The Little White Bird* (New York: Scribner's, 1902).

14. Andrew Birkin, *J. M. Barrie and the Lost Boys* (New Haven: Yale University Press, 2003), Introduction (n.p.).

15. Ibid.

16. Ibid.

17. Ibid.

18. Marjorie Garber, "Introduction: Postmodernism and the Possibil-

ity of Biography," in Mary Rhiel and David Suchoff, eds., *The Se-ductions of Biography* (New York: Routledge, 1996), p. 175.

19. Paula R. Backscheider, *Reflections on Biography* (Oxford: Oxford University Press, 1999), p. 164.

20. Janet Malcolm, *The Silent Woman* (New York: Knopf, 1994), pp. 8–9.

21. The court found against Masson in all but a negligible regard, and awarded him token damages of one penny.

22. From "The Dogs Are Eating Your Mother," in Ted Hughes, *Birthday Letters* (London: Faber and Faber, 1998), p. 195.

CHAPTER 13. BIOGRAPHY TODAY

1. Paula R. Backscheider, *Reflections on Biography* (Oxford: Oxford University Press, 1999), p. xiii.

2. Usually titled "life-writing" classes, most courses encouraged students to examine literature that focused on individual life experience, whether fictional or documentary; see, for example, David Cavitch, ed., *Life Studies: An Analytic Reader* (Boston: St. Martin's, 2001). It should be noted by aspiring students of biography, however, that the term "life studies" was and is a term more commonly applied to the practical, therapeutic, spiritual, and philosophical enhancement of human lives *through* biographical study, among other means. This method is used, for example, at the Center for Life Studies, Sunbridge College, in Spring Valley, New York, and at the College of Applied Life Studies, University of Illinois at Urbana-Champaign (which includes programs in Community Health, Kinesiology, Leisure Studies, and Speech and Hearing Science).

3. The "turn" in sociology in "reestablishing" the biographical rather than purely statistical method came in the last decade of the twentieth century. As Alan Bryman notes in his foreword to Brian Roberts, *Biographical Research* (Buckingham, U.K.: Open University Press, 2002), "In the last ten to fifteen years, the biographical method (as it is increasingly referred to) has become an extremely

significant approach to social research. This surge of interest in the method can be attributed to a variety of factors: a developing disillusionment with static approaches to data collection; a growing interest in the life course; an increased concern with 'lived experience' and how best to express and reveal it; and, of course, the method has shared in the growth in popularity of qualitative research in general" (p. x)—research that now involves ethnomethodology, phenomenology, narrative analysis, symbolic interactionism, discourse theory, conversational analysis, and other approaches.

Brian Roberts summarizes: "Despite philosophical, literary and other explorations of individuality, modern social sciences have tended to omit the 'humanity' of the individual," preferring to pursue "causal accounts, objective study of the general patterns of human behaviour and standard features of individuals drawn from natural science assumptions, procedures and principles. . . . The 'individuality' of individuals and the diversity of human meanings have been either neglected or relegated to a secondary concern (a residue)" (ibid., p. 4).

With the movement toward the "biographical method," however, the challenge that biographers faced for decades has at last been embraced by academic sociologists too, especially in their fieldwork. Roberts welcomes the change: "The appeal of biographical research is that it is exploring, in diverse methodological and interpretive ways, how individual accounts of life experience can be understood within the contemporary cultural and structural settings and is thereby helping to chart the major societal changes that are underway, but not merely at some broad social level. Biographical research has the important merit of aiding the task of understanding major social shifts, by including how new experiences are interpreted by individuals within families, small groups and institutions" (ibid., p. 5).

4. The only exceptions are the University of Hawaii at Manoa, which

started its Center for Biographical Research in the 1970s; La Trobe University in Melbourne, which founded a program in the 1990s; and a handful of smaller groups in places ranging from England to New Zealand, mostly devoted to life writing and autobiography.

La Trobe University established its Unit for Studies in Biography and Autobiography in 1996 as part of the English Program in the School of Communication, Arts and Critical Enquiry. In addition to teaching biography and autobiography, the unit functions as a center for biographical and autobiographical research. Monash University, near Melbourne, offers a Biographical and Life Writing Program as part of its School of Historical Studies. The University of Sussex, in England, opened its Centre for Life History Research in 1999, building on its Mass-Observation archives dating back to 1937. Similar units are being formed and developed as global interest in the research, theory, and teaching of biography and autobiography increases.

Sociologists, in particular, have shown renewed interest in the field. As Robert Miller says with regard to the four-volume work he edited, *Biographical Research Methods* (London: Sage, 2005): "The life history or biographical research method was popular in the early decades of the twentieth century and, after a period of eclipse caused by the rise of quantitative methods, is enjoying a resurgence of interest. This burgeoning of interest is enough that we can now speak of a biographical 'turn' in the social sciences." Book description at www.sagepub.com/booksProdDesc.nav?contribId= 504580&prodId=Book226923 (accessed September 2006).

5. The journal is *Biography,* an interdisciplinary quarterly published by the Center for Biographical Research since 1978, which is part of the College of Languages, Linguistics, and Literature at the University of Hawaii at Manoa. A&E Television Networks also publishes a commercial quarterly periodical titled *Biography,* launched in 1997, based on its very successful *Biography* cable channel.

More specialized academic journals devoted to the sociological and other aspects of autobiography and life writing have mushroomed. These include *Auto/Biography*, the bulletin of the British Sociological Association Study Group on Auto/Biography; *Auto/ Biography Studies: a/b*, a New York quarterly published since 1985; and *Life Writing*, an anthology issued by Massey University's School of Social and Cultural Studies, Auckland, New Zealand, published since 2003. French, German, and other language periodicals are also proliferating, with international conferences convening across the globe.

Masters programs in life writing are offered at numerous universities, though all too seldom within the framework of historical study of biography. Many teachers of life writing still admit, in fact, that they do not read or view biographies, nor are they interested in history or biography per se, beyond the narrow linguistic/ literary study of self-representation as a branch of English-literature studies.

6. Michiko Kakutani, "Bending the Truth in a Million Little Ways," *New York Times*, January 17, 2006, p. E1.

7. Marjorie Garber, "Introduction: Postmodernism and the Possibility of Biography," in Mary Rhiel and David Suchoff, eds., *The Seductions of Biography* (New York: Routledge, 1996), p. 175.

8. Backscheider, *Reflections on Biography*, p. 230.

9. Janet Malcolm, *The Silent Woman* (New York: Knopf, 1994), pp. 185–186.

10. Ibid., p. 9.

11. See Backscheider, *Reflections on Biography*, pp. 182–201.

12. Daniel S. Burt, *The Biography Book: A Reader's Guide to Nonfiction, Fictional, and Film Biographies of More Than 500 of the Most Fascinating Individuals of All Time* (Westport, Conn.: Oryx Press, 2001).

13. The comic strip is, in itself, a fascinating aspect of biography, with a long history. In recent years, comics have formed the basis for entire books and even films. Examples are Art Spiegelman's *Maus* (begun in 1971 and appearing in book form in the 1980s), Harvey

Pekar's *American Splendor* (started in 1976, filmed in 2003), and Alison Bechdel's *Fun Home* (2006).

14. William Zinsser, *Writing about Your Life: A Journey into the Past* (New York: Marlowe, 2005), p. 157.

15. "Truth and Memoir: A Conversation with William Zinsser," *Authors Guild Bulletin* (Spring 2006): 43.

16. Lily Koppel, "A Student, and a Glimpse through the Eyes of a Mentor," *New York Times,* April 8, 2006, p. A12.

17. "Truth and Memoir: A Conversation with William Zinsser," p. 43.

EPILOGUE

1. Frans de Waal, *Our Inner Ape* (New York: Riverhead, 2005), p. 94.

Bibliography

Following is a small selection of works relating to biography and non-fiction, in various media. It is intended to illustrate the range of published works devoted to the subject from myriad perspectives—literary, historical, archaeological, philosophical, psychological, women's studies, American studies, classical studies, film studies, media studies, and so on—all of which will help one day to inform a freestanding discipline of Biography and Life Study in the academy.

Altick, Richard D. *Lives and Letters: A History of Literary Biography in England and America*. New York: Knopf, 1966.

Anderson, Judith H. *Biographical Truth: The Representation of Historical Persons in Tudor-Stuart Writing*. New Haven: Yale University Press, 1984.

Appleby, Joyce, et al. *Telling the Truth about History*. New York: Norton, 1994.

Backscheider, Paula R. *Reflections on Biography*. Oxford: Oxford University Press, 1999.

Barnes, Julian. *Flaubert's Parrot*. London: Cape, 1984.

Barzun, Jacques. *The Interpretation of History*. Ed. Joseph R. Strayer. New York: Peter Smith, 1950.

Batchelor, John, ed. *The Art of Literary Biography*. Oxford: Clarendon, 1989.

Bell, Susan Groag, and Marilyn Yalom, eds. *Revealing Lives: Autobiography, Biography, and Gender*. Albany: State University of New York Press, 1990.

Birkin, Andrew. *J. M. Barrie and the Lost Boys*. New Haven: Yale University Press, 2003.

Bowen, Catherine Drinker. *Biography: The Craft and the Calling*. Boston: Little, Brown, 1969.

Boswell, James. *Boswell's Life of Johnson*. Ed. G. H. Hill. Oxford: Oxford University Press, 1934.

Bradford, Gamaliel. *Biography and the Human Heart*. Boston: Houghton Mifflin, 1932.

Burt, Daniel S. *The Biography Book: A Reader's Guide to Non-Fiction, Fictional and Film Biographies of More Than 500 of the Most Fascinating Individuals of All Time*. Westport, Conn.: Oryx Press, 2001.

Calvocoressi, Peter. *Who's Who in the Bible*. London: Viking, 1987.

Carr, Edward H. *What Is History?* New York: Vintage, 1961.

Caughie, John, ed. *Theories of Authorship: A Reader*. London: Routledge, 1981.

Clifford, James L., ed. *Biography as an Art: Selected Criticism, 1560–1960*. New York: Oxford University Press, 1962.

Cockshut, A. O. J. *The Art of Autobiography in Nineteenth- and Twentieth-Century England*. New Haven: Yale University Press, 1984.

Couser, G. Thomas. *American Autobiography: The Prophetic Mode*. Amherst: University of Massachusetts Press, 1979.

Custen, George F. *Bio/Pics: How Hollywood Constructed Public History*. New Brunswick, N.J.: Rutgers University Press, 1992.

Davenport, William H., and Ben Siegel, eds. *Biography Past and Present: Selections and Critical Essays*. New York: Scribner's, 1965.

Denzin, Norman K. *Interpretive Biography*. Thousand Oaks, Calif.: Sage, 1989.

Durling, Dwight Leonard, and William Watt, eds. *Biography: Varieties and Parallels*. New York: Dryden, 1941.

Eakin, Paul J. *Fictions in Autobiography: Studies in the Art of Self Invention*. Princeton: Princeton University Press, 1985.

——— *How Our Lives Become Stories: Making Selves*. Ithaca, N.Y.: Cornell University Press, 1999.

———— *Touching the World: Reference in Autobiography*. Princeton: Princeton University Press, 1992.

Eakin, Paul J., ed. *American Autobiography: Retrospect and Prospect*. Madison: University of Wisconsin Press, 1991.

———— *The Ethics of Life Writing*. Ithaca, N.Y.: Cornell University Press, 2004.

Edel, Leon. *Writing Lives: Principia Biographia*. New York: Norton, 1987.

Elms, Alan C. *Uncovering Lives: The Uneasy Alliance of Biography and Psychology*. New York: Oxford University Press, 1994.

Epstein, William H., ed. *Contesting the Subject: Essays in the Postmodern Theory and Practice of Biography and Biographical Criticism*. West Lafayette, Ind.: Perdue University Press, 1991.

Fay, Brian, et al. *History and Theory: Contemporary Readings*. Oxford: Blackwell, 1998.

Foucault, Michel. *The History of Sexuality*, vol. 1 (1976). Trans. Robert Hurley. New York: Vintage, 1980.

Freud, Sigmund. *Leonardo da Vinci and a Memory of His Childhood* (1910). Trans. Alan Tyson, ed. James Strachey. New York: Norton, 1961.

Gibbons, Randall, comp. *In Their Own Words*. New York: Random House, 1995.

Gilmore, Leigh. *Autobiographics: A Feminist Theory of Women's Self-Representation*. Ithaca, N.Y.: Cornell University Press, 1994.

Goodwin, James. *Autobiography: The Self Made Text*. New York: Twayne, 1993.

Hamilton, Ian. *Keepers of the Flame: Literary Estates and the Rise of Biography*. London: Hutchinson, 1992.

Hardt, Hanno. *Critical Communication Studies: Communication, History and Theory in America*. London: Routledge, 1992.

Holmes, Richard. *Footsteps: Adventures of a Romantic Biographer*. New York: Viking, 1985.

———— *Sidetracks: Explorations of a Romantic Biographer*. London: HarperCollins, 2000.

Holroyd, Michael. *Lytton Strachey: The New Biography*. London: Chatto and Windus, 1994.

Homberger, Eric, and John Charmley, eds. *The Troubled Face of Biography*. New York: St. Martin's, 1988.

Hughson, Lois. *From Biography to History: The Historical Imagination and American Fiction, 1880–1940*. Charlottesville: University Press of Virginia, 1988.

Iles, Theresa, ed. *All Sides of the Subject: Women and Biography*. New York: Teachers College Press, 1922.

Jolly, Margaretta, ed. *Encyclopedia of Life Writing: Autobiographical and Biographical Forms*. London: Fitzroy Dearborn, 2001.

Kendall, Paul Murray. *The Art of Biography*. London: Allen and Unwin, 1965.

Lejeune, Philippe. *Le Pacte Autobiographique*. Paris: Seuil, 1975.

——— *On Autobiography*. Minneapolis: University of Minnesota Press, 1989.

Lehman, Daniel W. *Matters of Fact: Reading Nonfiction over the Edge*. Columbus: Ohio State University Press, 1997.

MacDonald, Kevin, and Mark Cousins, eds. *Imagining Reality: The Faber Book of the Documentary*. London: Faber and Faber, 1996.

Malcolm, Janet. *The Silent Woman*. New York: Knopf, 1994.

Maurois, André. *Aspects of Biography*. New York: Appleton, 1929.

Merrill, Dana K. *American Biography: Its Theory and Practice*. Portland, Maine: Bowker, 1957.

Meyers, Jeffrey, ed. *The Craft of Literary Biography*. London: Macmillan, 1985.

Miller, Robert, ed. *Biographical Research Methods*. 4 vols. London: Sage, 2005.

Montaigne, Michel de. *Essays*. Trans. Donald M. Frame. Palo Alto: Stanford University Press, 1958.

Moraitis, George, and George H. Pollock, eds. *Psychoanalytic Studies of Biography*. Madison, Conn.: International Universities Press, 1987.

Morgan, J. R., and Richard Stoneman, eds. *Greek Fiction: The Greek Novel in Context*. London: Routledge, 1994.

Musser, Charles. *The Emergence of Cinema: The American Screen to 1907*. Berkeley: University of California Press, 1990.

Nadel, Ira Bruce. *Biography: Fiction, Fact and Form*. New York: St. Martin's, 1984.

Nicolson, Harold. *The Development of English Biography*. London: Hogarth, 1927.

Novarr, David. *The Lines of Life: Theories of Biography, 1880–1970*. West Lafayette, Ind.: Perdue University Press, 1986.

Oates, Stephen B., ed. *Biography as High Adventure: Life-Writers Speak on Their Art*. Amherst: University of Massachusetts Press, 1986.

O'Donnell, James J. *Augustine: The New Biography*. New York: Ecco, 2005.

Olney, James. *Memory and Narrative: The Weave of Life-Writing*. Chicago: University of Chicago Press, 1998.

———— *Metaphors of Self: The Meaning of Autobiography*. Princeton: Princeton University Press, 1972.

Olney, James, ed. *Autobiography: Essays Theoretical and Critical*. Princeton: Princeton University Press, 1980.

———— *Studies in Autobiography*. New York: Oxford University Press, 1998.

Pagels, Elaine. *The Gnostic Gospels*. New York: Vintage, 1979.

Parke, Catherine N. *Writing Lives*. New York: Twayne, 1996.

Plutarch. *The Lives of the Noble Grecians and Romans*. Trans. John Dryden, rev. Arthur Clough. New York: Modern Library, 1979.

Powell, John, ed. *Victorian Biography*. Special issue of *Nineteenth-Century Prose*, vol. 22, no. 2 (Fall 1995).

Raleigh, Sir Walter. *The History of the World*. Ed. C. A. Patrides. Philadelphia: Temple University Press, 1971.

Reid, B. L. *Necessary Lives: Biographical Reflections*. Columbia: University of Missouri Press, 1990.

Renov, Michael, ed. *Theorizing Documentary*. London: Routledge, 1993.

Rhiel, Mary, and David Suchoff, eds. *The Seductions of Biography*. New York: Routledge, 1996.

Roberts, Brian. *Biographical Research*. Buckingham, U.K.: Open University Press, 2002.

Rollyson, Carl E. *Biography: An Annotated Bibliography*. Magill Bibliographies. Pasadena: Salem, 1992.

—— *A Higher Form of Capitalism? Adventures in the Art and Politics of Biography*. Chicago: Ivan R. Dee, 2005.

Royle, Nicholas, ed. *Deconstructions: A User's Guide*. Basingstoke, U.K.: Palgrave, 2000.

Rubin, William. *Picasso and Portraiture: Representation and Transformation*. New York: Museum of Modern Art, 1996.

Schaffer, Kay, and Sidonie Smith. *Human Rights and Narrated Lives: The Ethics of Recognition*. New York: Palgrave Macmillan, 2004.

Smith, Sidonie. *Subjectivity, Identity and the Body: Women's Autobiographical Practices in the Twentieth Century*. Bloomington: Indiana University Press, 1993.

—— *A Poetics of Women's Autobiography: Marginality and the Fictions of Self-Representation*. Bloomington: Indiana University Press, 1987.

—— *Where I'm Bound: Patterns of Slavery and Freedom in Black American Autobiography*. Westport, Conn.: Greenwood, 1974.

Smith, Sidonie, and Julia Watson, eds. *Interfaces: Women, Autobiography, Image, Performance*. Ann Arbor: University of Michigan Press, 2002.

—— *Reading Autobiography: A Guide for Interpreting Life Narratives*. Minneapolis: University of Minnesota Press, 2001.

—— *Women, Autobiography, Theory: A Reader*. Madison: University of Wisconsin Press, 1998.

—— *Getting a Life: Everyday Uses of Autobiography*. Minneapolis: University of Minnesota, 1996.

—— *De/Colonizing the Subject: The Politics of Gender in Women's Autobiography*. Minneapolis: University of Minnesota Press, 1992.

Stauffer, Donald A. *English Biography before 1700*. Cambridge, Mass.: Harvard University Press, 1930.

Strachey, Lytton. *Eminent Victorians* (1918). Harmondsworth: Penguin, 1986.

Suetonius. *The Twelve Caesars*. Trans. Robert Graves. Harmondsworth: Penguin, 1957. Revised 1979, ed. Michael Grant.

Thompson, Paul. *The Voice of the Past: Oral History*. Oxford: Oxford University Press, 1988.

Turner, A. Richard. *Inventing Leonardo: The Anatomy of a Legend*. New York: Knopf, 1993.

Waal, Frans de. *Our Inner Ape*. New York: Riverhead Books, 2005.

Walker, Susan, and Morris Bierbrier. *Ancient Faces: Mummy Portraits from Roman Egypt*. London: British Museum Press, 1997.

Wendorf, Richard. *The Elements of Life: Biography and Portrait-Painting in Stuart and Georgian England*. Oxford: Clarendon, 1990.

Wheeler, David, ed. *Domestick Privacies: Samuel Johnson and the Art of Biography*. Lexington: University Press of Kentucky, 1987.

Whittemore, Reed. *Pure Lives: The Early Biographers*. Baltimore: Johns Hopkins University Press, 1988.

———— *Whole Lives: Shapers of Modern Biography*. Baltimore: Johns Hopkins University Press, 1989.

Wilson, Ian. *Jesus: The Evidence*. London: Weidenfeld and Nicolson, 1996.

Young-Bruehl, Elisabeth. *Subject to Biography: Psychoanalysis, Feminism, and Writing Women's Lives*. Cambridge, Mass.: Harvard University Press, 1988.

Zinsser, William. *Inventing the Truth: The Art and Craft of Memoir*. Boston: Houghton Mifflin, 1987, 1995, 1998.

———— *Writing about Your Life: A Journey into the Past*. New York: Marlowe, 2005.

Acknowledgments

*I*n the 1990s, while directing the British Institute of Biography (BiB) in London, and attempting to set up a national center for the study and celebration of biography, I was privileged to work with many distinguished biographers, academic colleagues, professionals, and financial sponsors. They opened my naïve eyes to the sheer *range* of biographical output in modern Western culture, from public art to museum exhibitions, genealogy to gerontology, history of science to electronic blogs. Had we been able to create such a national center—in the same way that the National Portrait Gallery was founded in the mid-nineteenth century—the public recognition of biography in Britain would have been greatly enhanced. I hope this small book reflects, at least, the passion that went into the six years of trying—though its brevity and limited scope do scant justice to such a fascinating interdisciplinary and international subject.

Among the many who deserve mention are those who were my fellow BiB trustees in the 1990s: biographers Michael Holroyd and Lady Antonia Fraser, *Dictionary of Na-*

tional Biography editor Christine Nicolls, and television documentary producer Jeremy Bennett. George Simson and Craig Howes, at the Center for Biographical Research at the University of Hawaii, lent international support to the project from afar. Sam Pitroda, father of the information technology revolution in India, financially sponsored the attempt to create a biographical Internet site (real-lives.com) to train University of London students in multimedia biographical research, compilation, and writing. My indefatigable assistant, Garth Davies, worked devotedly to realize the dream, and we were backed by an advisory board who stood behind the project throughout—including filmmakers Lord Attenborough and Lord Brabourne, former Education Secretary Lord Baker, Victoria and Albert Museum director Alan Borg, psychiatrist Anthony Clare, Imperial War Museum director Robert Crawford, cardiologist Sir Terence English, environmental scientist David Hall, former Defence Minister Lord Healey, genealogist Sir Malcolm Innes, school principal Michael Marland, *New Dictionary of National Biography* editor H. C. G. Matthew, British Museum librarian Andrew Phillips, university chancellor Baroness Prashar, economist Lord Roll, philosopher Baroness Warnock, and director of BBC network television Will Wyatt. I will not easily forget, either, the professionals who worked so hard on the team to plan the center, raise funds, and advance the scheme, including architect Sir Richard MacCormack, exhibition designer Steve Simons, and museum designer Geoff Marsh. One day, such a center will be built—and the work done on its creation will not have been for nothing.

My personal history of biographical involvement goes back a lifetime. I'd like to thank, especially, my mother, Olive Hamilton, who first instilled in me a love of historical personality and coauthored my first book, *Royal Greenwich;* my late wife, Hannelore, who inspired me to write my first major biography, *The Brothers Mann;* my late father, Sir Denis Hamilton, who guided me through the ten-year process of researching and writing *Monty,* my three-volume official biography of Field Marshal Montgomery of Alamein; my Cambridge University companion Robin Whitby, who partnered me in briefly establishing, in the 1980s, a small biographical reprint publishing house, Biografia Publishers Ltd., and a specialist bookstore, the Biography Bookshop, in London's Covent Garden; Jeremy Bennett, who produced and directed my first major BBC biographical television documentary, *Monty: In Love and War,* which won the New York Blue Ribbon Award; the University of Massachusetts at Boston, which awarded me the John F. Kennedy Scholarship in 1988 when I embarked on my life of JFK; my colleagues in the UMass History

Department—especially Clive Foss, Paul Bookbinder, Malcolm Smuts, and Bill Percy—where I taught a post-graduate biographical history course on the life and times of America's thirty-fifth president; and above all my colleagues at the McCormack Institute of Public Affairs, of which I was a fellow for six years, while researching and writing *JFK: Reckless Youth*—especially the founding director, Ed Beard.

Resettling in Britain in 1994, I extended my teaching to the wider history of twentieth-century Western biography through the invitation of my colleagues in the Department of History at Royal Holloway, University of London. I remain indebted to them—especially Francis Robinson and Claudia Liebeskind—as well as to the college for its contribution toward establishing a national center for biography at Royal Holloway's beautiful Egham campus in Surrey.

Moving to the Faculty of Humanities at De Montfort University, I became Professor of Biography, and taught a Masters course in military biography while revising my three-volume life of Montgomery for Allen Lane, Penguin Press, as *The Full Monty*. I thank especially Julia Briggs, Judy Simons, David Sadler, Mark Sandle, Peter Robinson, George Rousseau, and Nigel Wood for their assistance, and to David Brunnen for his help in further exploring the project for a biography center at De Montfort, and the effort to obtain funding for, at minimum, a virtual biographical center via the New Opportunities Fund.

With the failure of this effort in Britain, I returned to the United States in order to write *Bill Clinton: An American Journey,* a multivolume biography of the forty-second president. I'd like to acknowledge the support of the staff and fellows of the renamed McCormack Graduate School of Policy Studies at the University of Massachusetts, Boston, where I resettled in 2000. To Acting Dean Ed Beard, Founding Dean Steve Crosby, and Assistant Dean Sandy Blanchette, to staffers Candyce Carragher, Jamie Ennis, and Mike McPhee, and to all my fellow fellows and colleagues in the new school, my sincere gratitude. Without their assistance and goodwill, I would not be able to practice what I teach.

Last, I must acknowledge my gratitude to my life-partner, Raynel Shepard, who, in the midst of my labors on the life of Bill Clinton, suggested that I approach her alma mater, Harvard University, with regard to this brief sketch of biography's long and sometimes difficult history. At Harvard University Press, Joyce Seltzer saw merit in the manuscript that I sent her, despite its many flaws, and guided it through to publication; Maria Ascher ironed out a thousand infelicities. For its sins of omission, its Anglocentricity, its Western compass, and its broad-brush simplification of a complex history, I bear the entire blame. I hope that, despite these shortcomings, it will prove useful and inspiring to students, practitioners, and fellow aficionados of life depiction in all its forms.

Index